10 Minute Guide to

The Internet with Windows® 95

by Galen A. Grimes

A Division of Macmillan Computer Publishing
201 West 103rd St., Indianapolis, Indiana 46290 USA

©1995 by Que® Corporation

All rights reserved. No part of this book shall be reproduced, stored in a retrieval system, or transmitted by any means, electronic, mechanical, photocopying, recording, or otherwise, without written permission from the publisher. No patent liability is assumed with respect to the use of the information contained herein. Although every precaution has been taken in the preparation of this book, the publisher and author assume no responsibility for errors or omissions. Neither is any liability assumed for damages resulting from the use of the information contained herein. For information, address Que Corporation, 201 W. 103rd Street, Indianapolis, IN 46290. You can reach Que's direct sales line by calling 1-800-428-5331.

International Standard Book Number: 0-7897-0663-6
Library of Congress Catalog Card Number: 95-71744

97 96 95   3 2 1

Interpretation of the printing code: the rightmost number of the first series of numbers is the year of the book's printing; the rightmost number of the second series of numbers is the number of the book's printing. For example, a printing code of 95-1 shows that the first printing of the book occurred in 1995.

Screen reproductions in this book were created by means of the program Collage Plus from Inner Media, Inc., Hollis, NH.

Printed in the United States of America

President
Roland Elgey

Publisher, New Technologies
Stacy Hiquet

Senior Series Editor
Chris Nelson

Director of Editorial Services
Elizabeth Keaffaber

Managing Editor
Sandy Doell

Director of Marketing
Lynn E. Zingraf

Title Manager
Jim Minatel

Acquisitions Editor
Beverly M. Eppink

Product Director
Benjamin Milstead

Production Editor
Danielle Bird

Copy Editor
Noelle Gasco

Technical Editors
Jeff Bankston, Greg Newman

Book Designer
Kim Scott

Cover Designer
Dan Armstrong

Operations Coordinator
Patricia J. Brooks

Editorial Assistant
Andrea Duvall

Acquisitions Assistant
Ruth Slates

Production Team
Brian Buschkill, Joan Evan, Michelle Lee, Julie Quinn, Scott Tullis, Paul Wilson, Karen York

Indexer
Brad Herriman

Acknowledgments

Special thanks to the book-building team: Beverly Eppink, Ben Milstead, Danielle Bird, Noelle Gasco, Andrea Duvall, Ruth Slates, Jeff Bankston, Greg Newman and all the folks in Proofreading and Layout. None of this would have been possible without your long hours and patience with me. And a very special thanks to Bev and Ben who struggled through my incessant revisions.

Dedication

To my older brothers Rod and Brod who helped me find so much about life as we were growing up. I hope this helps them find the Internet.

Contents

Introduction   viii

1 Finding Out About the Internet   1
    What Is the Internet? 1
    What You Need To Get Started 3

2 Selecting an Internet Service Provider   7
    What Is Internet Service? 7
    You Can Get Access Through Your Online Service 7
    About Internet Service Provider Shell Accounts 8
    What Are Internet Service Provider SLIP/PPP Accounts? 9
    Selecting an Internet Service Provider 10

3 Installing the Windows 95 TCP/IP Client   13
    What Is the Windows 95 TCP/IP Client? 13

4 Configuring the Windows 95 PPP/SLIP Connection   18
    Setting Up the SLIP/PPP Connection 18

5 Setting Up Windows 95 with Dial-Up Networking   23
    How To Set Up Dial-Up Networking 23

6 Using the Internet Setup Wizard   27
    Installing Microsoft Plus! 27
    Running the Internet Setup Wizard 29

7 Using Dial-Up Networking To Get on the Internet   35
    Connecting to the Internet 35

8 Using the Windows 95 FTP Utility   40
    What Is the Windows 95 FTP? 40
    Using FTP 41

9 Using a Windows-Based FTP Utility— WS_FTP32 46

Installing WS_FTP32 46
Running WS_FTP32 47

10 Sending Email with Microsoft Exchange 51

Configuring MS Exchange 51
Keeping Track with Your Address Book 52
Creating and Sending Email 54
Receiving Email 56
Other Internet Email Programs 58

11 Discovering the World Wide Web 60

What Is the World Wide Web? 60
Netscape Navigator 60
Discovering the Web 62
Netscape's History and Bookmarks Features 67

12 Using Microsoft Internet Explorer 68

Microsoft's Internet Explorer 68
Using Internet Explorer 70

13 Setting Bookmarks and Marking Favorite Pages 79

Using Netscape's Bookmarks 79
Recording Your Favorite Pages in Internet Explorer 84

14 Searching the Internet Using Search Engines 88

What Is a Search Engine? 88
Yahoo 88
Lycos 95

15 Viewing and Using Graphic Files on the Internet 99

Viewing Graphic Files 99

16 Audio on the Internet—Audio and RealAudio™   105

Audio on the Internet 105
RealAudio™ 107

17 Adding File Types in MS Internet Explorer   112

Configuring File Types in Internet Explorer 112
Obtaining an MPEG Viewer 113
Associating the File Type MPEG/MPG 114
Displaying MPEG Files with Internet Explorer 115

18 Configuring Helper Apps for Netscape   117

Setting Up Netscape To Use Helper Apps 117
Obtaining the QuickTime Viewer 118
Configuring Netscape To Use QuickTime 119
Displaying QuickTime Movies with Netscape 119

19 How UseNet Newsgroups Work   123

What Are UseNet Newsgroups? 123
How Newsgroups Are Organized 124
What You Need 125
What You See 126

20 Setting Up and Using a Newsreader   128

Acquiring and Setting Up Your Newsreader 128
Reading News Articles 131

21 Subscribing and Posting to a Newsgroup   135

Subscribing to a Newsgroup 135
Posting a Newsgroup Article 136

22 Decoding and Viewing UseNet Graphic Files   140

UseNet Graphic Files 140

23 REAL-TIME CHAT ON THE INTERNET — 145

What Is Internet Relay Chat? 145
IRC Client Software 145
Getting and Configuring Worlds Chat 146
Running Worlds Chat 148
Other IRC Client Programs 151

24 GOPHERING ON THE INTERNET — 153

What Is Gopher? 153
Using a Gopher Client Program 153
Using HGopher 154
Searching Gopherspace 156

25 GOPHERING WITH VERONICA — 160

Using Veronica To Do Gopher Searches 160

26 TELNETTING TO MULTI-USER DOMAINS — 165

Multi-User Domains 165
Playing a MUD 165
Adding a New Dimension to Multi-Dimension 168

27 CONNECTING THROUGH THE MICROSOFT NETWORK — 169

What Is The Microsoft Network? 169
Subscribing to MSN 170
Pros and Cons of Accessing the Internet Through MSN 172

A CREATING A SCRIPT FOR DIAL-UP NETWORKING — 174

Creating Your Dial-Up Script 175

INDEX — 179

INTRODUCTION

Do you know where you can find:

- The current U.S. census
- The FBI's Ten Most Wanted list
- Schedules of all NCAA Division I football and basketball teams
- Pictures of Mt. Everest and Mt. K2
- Information on certain types and brands of inline skates
- What movies are playing in your city this weekend
- How many Cokes are left in the soda machine on the 7th floor of Watson at Columbia University
- Which actors have portrayed Romulans on *Star Trek: The Next Generation*
- What research studies have been conducted on asthma in the last 10 years
- The price of the Doors CD Morrison Hotel

If you haven't guessed by now, the answer is: You can find all of these things on the Internet, and without leaving the comfort of your favorite chair.

In the past few years, the Internet has experienced phenomenal growth, not only in the amount of information and services available online, but also in the number of people accessing that information. But there's more to the Internet than just information, facts, and figures.

The Internet has been invaded by entertainment promoters and entrepeneurs. Hundreds of businesses are now investigating ways of getting names and products online because of the potential audience they can reach.

It seems that everyone wants to get onboard the Internet express. A year or two ago it seemed that it took a doctoral degree in computer science to figure out the vagaries of connecting to the Internet. You had to know UNIX and how to setup and configure TCP/IP protocol stacks, SLIP/PPP connections, and IP addresses. Thank goodness those days are long gone.

Welcome to the *10 Minute Guide to the Internet with Windows 95*!

On the surface, the idea of combining a new 32-bit operating system with an Internet connection may seem like your worst computer nightmare, but as you will soon see, it's as easy as falling off a log. The *10 Minute Guide to the Internet with Windows 95* takes a straightforward, easy-to-understand approach to guiding you through every aspect of setting up your connection, and getting you to the Internet, and then shows you what you can do once you get there.

This book is for anyone interested in...

- Understanding how to establish an Internet account
- Using Windows 95 to access and discover the Internet
- Locating information and entertainment on the World Wide Web
- What a Web browser is and how to use one to access the most popular aspect of the Internet

How To Use This Book

The "essential" lessons in this book are Lessons 1-7. They explain how to connect to the Internet. The remaining lessons explain various aspects of Windows 95 and the Internet. Depending on your level of expertise in using the Internet, you may or may not find these lessons useful. If you're still an Internet beginner, by all means continue with Lesson 8 on through to the end of this book. While some points may be a repeat of information you may already know, or may have read in another text, chances are you will find a lot of helpful information as you explore the Net. If you are a more experienced Net hound, you should still take the time to browse through lessons that pertain to parts of the Internet you're already familiar with. You will probably find some of the tips included in each lesson helpful.

Conventions Used in This Book

You'll find icons throughout this book to help you save time and learn important information fast:

Timesaver Tips These give you insider hints for using the Internet with Windows 95.

Plain English These icons call your attention to definitions of new terms.

Panic Button Look to these icons for warnings and cautions about potential problem areas.

You'll also find common conventions for steps you will perform:

What you type — Things you type will appear in bold, color type.

Press Enter — Any keys you press or items you select with your mouse will appear in color type.

On-screen text	Any on-screen messages you will see will appear in bold type.
Press Alt+F1	Any key combinations you must press simultaneously will appear in this format.
New Terms	Any new terms appear in bold type.
URLs	Addresses appear in bold, color type.
Names of fields and areas	Names of fields and areas on-screen appear in bold in places where you are to directed to them.

TRADEMARKS

All terms mentioned in this book that are known to be trademarks have been appropriately capitalized. Que Corporation cannot attest to the accuracy of this information. Use of a term in this book should not be regarded as affecting the validity of any trademark or service mark.

Finding Out About the Internet

In this lesson, you learn what the Internet is and what you can do on it using Windows 95.

What Is the Internet?

If you've watched the news much in the past year, undoubtedly you've noticed all the hoopla over the Internet. Although the Internet, or its forerunner ARPANET, has been around since the late 1960s, you would think that the worldwide network of computers magically became connected during the last year. The Internet has been the hot topic lately, and it doesn't seem likely that the topic will cool down in the future.

The Internet's popularity has fueled the demand for books, like this one, designed to help ease you into what at first must seem like a technological hodgepodge. The Internet may at first seem insurmountable. By the time you finish this book, however, you'll think of yourself as an Internet expert. You'll understand Web browsers and TCP/IP stacks, Gophers and SLIP connections, and you will likely be showing other, less informed users how to access search engines and FTP servers.

Access to the Internet is, foremost, access to a wealth of information, from academic research to stock market quotes to information on hang gliding and inline skating (see Figures 1.1 and 1.2). You can do geographical and geological research, and you can review Casey Kasem's weekly Hit List (see Figure 1.3).

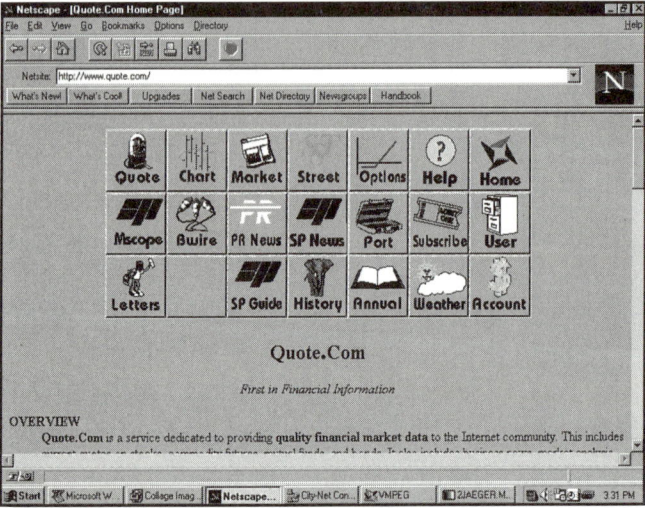

FIGURE 1.1 Quote.Com financial service.

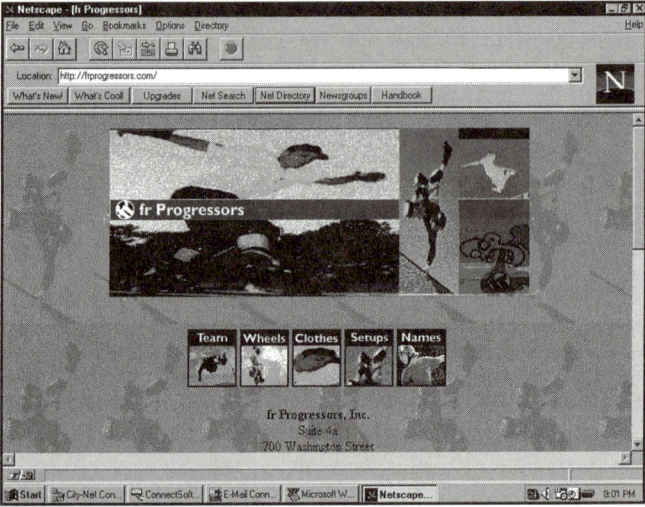

FIGURE 1.2 Inline skating on the Web.

Finding Out About the Internet 3

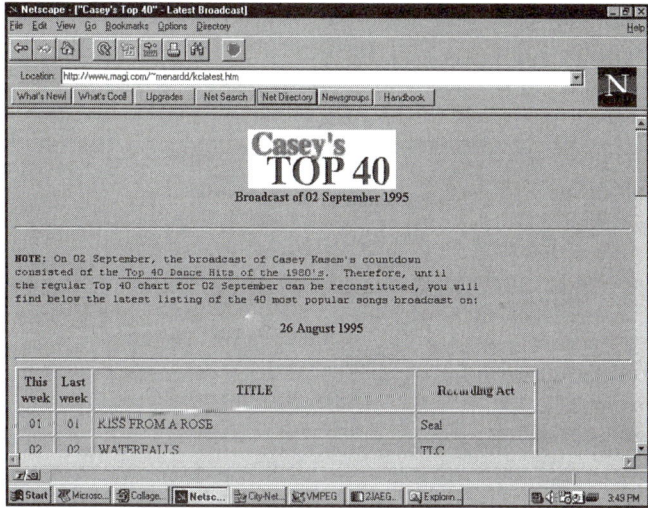

Figure 1.3 Casey's Top 40.

Originally designed as an academic-exchange medium, the Internet has become a favorite target of burgeoning entrepreneurs who sell everything from stocks, bonds, and mutual funds to CDs, music boxes, and vintage wines.

The Internet's access and appeal have also naturally caught the attention of most major computer hardware and software manufacturers and vendors. They've found that the Internet, or "the Net" as many old-timers call it, is an excellent way to reach and provide information and upgrades to their customer base and potential customer base. Besides Intel, as you see in Figure 1.4, other well known computer vendors with a presence on the Net include IBM, Compaq, Novell, Apple, and of course Microsoft.

What You Need To Get Started

Obviously, you need to have Windows 95 installed on your computer. This book is designed to help users who access the Internet directly through an Internet Service Provider (ISP), not through a local area network (LAN) that has an Internet **gateway**. For information on configuring on a LAN, talk to your system administrator.

FIGURE 1.4   Intel home page.

 **Gateway**   A gateway is pretty much what its name suggests. It's a means of "passing through" or "connecting to" a system different from the one you are using. An Internet gateway for a local area network is merely a means of providing Internet access to users on a LAN.

You also need an Internet account with an Internet Service Provider (ISP). If you don't have an Internet account yet, see Lesson 2, which explains how to select an ISP.

You also need a means of communicating with your service provider. This book assumes that your connection is over a standard telephone line using a modem. For acceptable performance, you need a modem capable of communicating at a rate of at least

14,400 bits per second (bps). People often refer to these modems as **14.4** (fourteen-dot-four) or **V.42** (vee-dot-forty-two). A slower modem doesn't provide an acceptable performance level for accessing graphical images over the Internet. A 28.8 modem gives the best performance over standard phone lines.

V.42 V.42 is the international specification for 14.4 (asynchronous) modem communications. Communications organizations from all over the world meet on a regular basis to decide communications specifications. These specifications dictate how hardware devices are to perform when communicating certain types of signals at certain speeds. The specification for 28.8 modem communications is V.34.

Another communication technology that looks to have a big impact on Internet usage is **ISDN**. ISDN (Integrated Services Digital Network) is literally "digital telephones." Rather than convert your computer's digital signals into analog (sound waves) to be transmitted over standard telephone lines, ISDN transmits a digital signal over digital telephone lines. The advantage is a communication connection up to 128 kilobits per second (kbps) as opposed to today's 28.8-kbps connections.

Windows 95 provides all the software you need to connect to the Internet. You may have heard that you need the Windows 95 bonus package, Microsoft Plus!, to gain Internet access. Microsoft Plus! provides a collection of additional utilities and programs for Windows 95, including the Internet Setup Wizard. The Internet Setup Wizard makes it easier to connect to the Internet but is not essential. This book explains how to connect to the Internet, both with and without Microsoft Plus!.

If you're not sure if all or part of Microsoft Plus! has been installed on your computer, here's how you can tell:

1. Select the Start button on the taskbar and choose Programs Windows Explorer.

LESSON 1

2. On your C:\ drive, locate a folder labeled **Plus!**. If you don't see this folder, most likely none of Microsoft Plus! has been installed on your PC, or at least on your C:\ drive (if you have more than one drive, check the others, too). If you do see the folder **Plus!**, check to see if the Internet Tools have been installed in a folder called **Microsoft Internet**.

3. Open the Start menu and choose Programs, Accessories. If your Accessories menu contains an Internet Tools option, choose Internet Tools to see if you have the Internet Setup Wizard installed (see Figure 1.5).

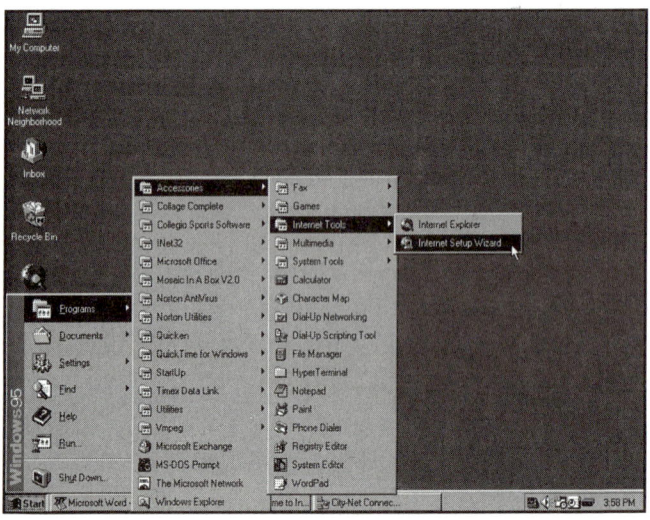

FIGURE 1.5 The Internet Setup Wizard installed.

In this lesson, you learned what the Internet is and what you need to get connected. In the next lesson, you learn how to select an Internet Service Provider (ISP).

LESSON 2
SELECTING AN INTERNET SERVICE PROVIDER

In this lesson, you learn how to select an Internet Service Provider (ISP).

WHAT IS INTERNET SERVICE?

Internet access comes in a variety of connection choices and account types depending on who provides the service and what hardware and software you use. This book examines the service options available to users with stand-alone computers, rather than the options available to users who have Internet access through a local area network (LAN).

Stand-Alone Computer A stand-alone computer is a computer that is not directly connected to another computer or computer system, such as a local area network. To access other computers, users with stand-alone computers usually use a modem to connect over ordinary telephone lines.

YOU CAN GET ACCESS THROUGH YOUR ONLINE SERVICE

Many of the commercial online services, such as CompuServe, America Online, Prodigy, and now Microsoft Network offer Internet access. Internet access through these services is usually quick and easy to set up, but the "meter is running" every minute you are connected. You can buy a month of unlimited Internet access from an "ordinary" Internet service provider for what commercial online services charge for less than 10 hours of Internet access. As a rough guideline, for many Internet Service Providers the going rate now is a month of unlimited connect time for around $20-30.

Commercial online service providers counter with the argument that they offer a wide array of additional services (vendor forums, email, file/program downloading, chat rooms, and so on)—all neatly organized and easily accessed through a familiar or easy-to-learn interface. However, once you become familiar with the Internet, you will find that most, if not all, of these services are available at a fraction of the cost. You only need to know where to look.

The questions here are, "How much time do you plan to spend on the Internet each month?," and "What is it worth to you to have these services laid out for you in a nice, neat little package?"

About Internet Service Provider Shell Accounts

Most Internet Service Providers have abandoned **shell accounts**, but these accounts are still available—usually at rock-bottom prices. Shell accounts come cheaply because they are text-only. In a world of Graphical User Interfaces (GUIs) and multimedia razzle-dazzle, few users are satisfied with surfing the Net with a text-only view.

On the plus side, a text-only interface does have one major advantage—speed! When you eliminate pictures, graphical fonts, and colors, you can access the Internet very quickly. In later lessons, you will see how you can turn off graphics mode at times when you want to surf the Net at warp speed rather than cruise on impulse power.

What Are Internet Service Provider SLIP/PPP Accounts?

Serial Line Internet Protocol (SLIP) and **Point-to-Point Protocol (PPP)** are two types of Internet accounts most users presently turn to. SLIP is the older of the two types of Internet connections explained here. As its name implies, SLIP allows you to connect to a service provider over a serial communication line, such as a telephone line. Developed after SLIP, PPP is also serial in nature, but it provides a higher degree of error detection and compression in its connection to your service provider. When given a choice, choose PPP.

Still relatively inexpensive in most areas (especially compared to commercial networks), these accounts offer you Internet access through graphical interfaces and allow you to experience the full depth of the Internet and its services (see Figure 2.1). One of the goals of this book is to show you how to set up SLIP and PPP accounts, beginning in Lesson 4.

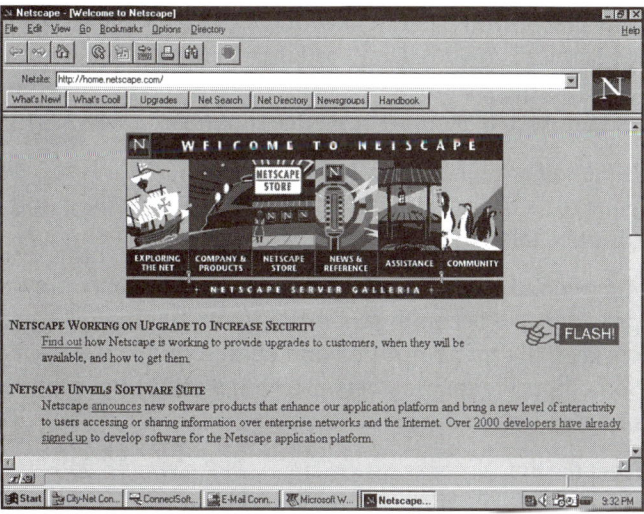

Figure 2.1 A popular way to surf the Net is to use Netscape.

Error detection Error detection is a built-in method of resending a communications signal if errors are detected between the source and recipient. SLIP connections get error detection from an outside source, often hardware. Today's high-speed modems assist by providing extra error detection, also.

Compression Compression is the process of encoding communication signals so that they can be sent as shorter signals and thereby take less time to send.

SELECTING AN INTERNET SERVICE PROVIDER

Now that you know something about the types of Internet accounts available, you need to know how to go about selecting an Internet Service Provider. Don't attempt to make the determination solely on the basis of price. Consider the following service options and discuss them with service providers:

- *Is the call to your ISP a local call?* The whole idea is to keep your costs to a minimum, which includes avoiding long-distance telephone charges.

- *Are you charged by the minute/hour or on a flat rate?* Flat-rate providers are becoming more common, but many providers keep the meter running and charge you by the hour. Some hourly rate providers give you a minimum number of hours before the meter starts.

- *Does the provider offer shell, SLIP, or PPP accounts?* PPP is the best type of connectivity for your money.

- *How many incoming telephone lines does your service provider make available?* The least-expensive provider is no longer a bargain if all you get when you dial-in is a busy signal.

- *What communication speeds do your service provider offer?* You set your modem to this speed to communicate with your providers' modems. Hardly any service providers offer speeds less than 14,400 bits per second (bps). If you're using a modem with a top speed of 28,800 bps, make sure your provider has phone lines that talk to your modem at this speed. If you think you might upgrade to ISDN connections sometime in the future, inquire whether your provider can provide these connections.

ISDN ISDN stands for Integrated Services Digital Network. The modems you use now communicate by converting the digital signal from your computer to an **analog signal**. In other words, your modem converts bits and bytes to sound and then transmits this analog signal over standard telephone lines. ISDN communicates as a **digital signal**, which means it does not use a "standard" modem, and thus is a lot faster—the signal doesn't have to be converted. ISDN speeds are either 64,000 bps over each of its 2 channels, or two combined 64-kilobyte-per-second signals into one 128-kbps signal provider supports combining, or **duplexing**, the two ISDN channels into the maximum transmission rate.

- *Does your service provider offer email, newsgroups, an online chat service? Can you browse the World Wide Web, and send and receive files through FTP? Can you use Telnet and Gopher?* In the coming lessons, you learn about these capabilities and what you can do with them. For now, just know that your provider should offer them all.

A service provider should offer at least those services listed in the preceding list. Some service providers go further and make shareware software and technical support available.

If you're wondering how to find an Internet provider, look for ads in online magazines, check the yellow pages, or simply ask someone about their provider.

Also, if you want to "sample the goods," many state-run universities have started providing Internet-access terminals in student union buildings and libraries where anyone can literally walk in off the street and get on the Internet.

In this lesson, you learned what questions to ask when selecting an Internet Service Provider. In the next three lessons, you learn how to configure Windows 95 to access the Internet through your provider. In the next lesson, you begin by learning how to install what is called the **TCP/IP protocol client**.

Installing the Windows 95 TCP/IP Client

Lesson 3

In this lesson, you learn how to install the Windows 95 TCP/IP client.

Use the Internet Setup Wizard! If you purchased Microsoft Plus!, you can use the Internet Setup Wizard to set up your Internet connection. Skip to Lesson 6 to use this Wizard. Be aware of one caveat, though: The Internet Setup Wizard works only if your Internet Service Provider supplies you with a PPP connection.

What Is the Windows 95 TCP/IP Client?

One reason for the success of the Internet is that all computers on the Internet are able to use the same protocol. A **protocol** is an agreed-upon means of communication, like a language. **Transmission Control Protocol/Internet Protocol (TCP/IP)** is the language spoken by all Internet computers and the language (protocol) your computer must also speak or use in order to access the Internet.

Client A client is something that is dependent on the services of another, usually a server; in this case, your TCP/IP client is dependent on the (Internet) TCP/IP server for communication.

14   LESSON 3

INSTALLING THE WINDOWS 95 TCP/IP CLIENT

Windows 95 includes the Internet protocol TCP/IP. Before you can access the Internet, you must install the Windows 95 TCP/IP client.

>  **Connect Quickly with Microsoft Plus!** If you purchased the Windows 95 add-on, Microsoft Plus!, you can skip this lesson plus Lessons 4 and 5, and proceed to Lesson 6.

Here's how you install the Windows 95 TCP/IP client:

1. Select the Start button on the taskbar and choose Settings, Control Panel to open the Control Panel window (see Figure 3.1).

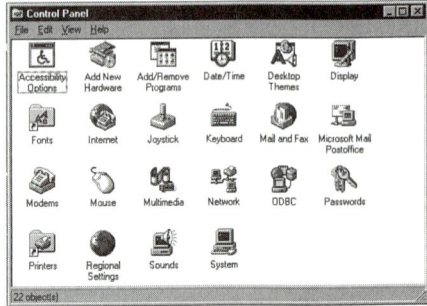

FIGURE 3.1   Windows 95 Control Panel.

2. Double-click Network to open the Network dialog box (see Figure 3.2).

3. Select the Add button. In the Select Network Component Type dialog box, double-click Client to open the Select Network Client dialog box (see Figure 3.3).

Installing the Windows 95 TCP/IP Client   15

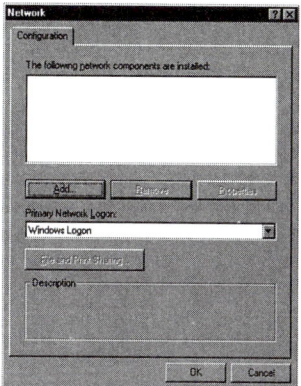

Figure 3.2 Network dialog box.

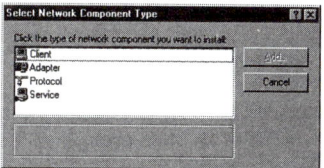

Figure 3.3 Select Network Component Type dialog box.

4. In the Manufacturers list, select (highlight) Microsoft. In the Network Clients list, double-click Client for Microsoft Networks. When the Select Device dialog box appears, choose OK.

This procedure installs the Client for Microsoft Networks, which must be installed before you can install TCP/IP. When you install the Client, Windows 95 also installs a few extra network services. Later in this lesson, you will delete these because they aren't needed for your stand-alone Internet connection.

Now you can install Windows 95 TCP/IP:

1. The Network dialog box should still be on-screen. If it's not, open the Control Panel window and select Network.

Select the Add button to open the Select Network Component Type dialog box.

2. Double-click Protocol. When the Select Network Protocol dialog box appears, select Microsoft from the Manufacturers list, and then double-click TCP/IP in the Network Protocols list. This takes you back to the Network dialog box and shows you that TCP/IP is now installed (see Figure 3.4).

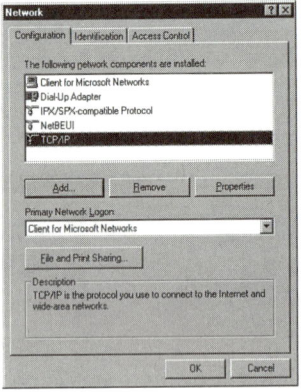

FIGURE 3.4   Network dialog box showing TCP/IP is installed.

Finally, you need to install the Dial-Up Adapter because you will be dialing in to your service provider:

1. In the Network dialog box, select the Add button.
2. In the Select Network Component Type dialog box, double-click Adapter.
3. In the Select Network Adapters dialog box, in the Manufacturers list, scroll down and select Microsoft. In the Network Adapters list, double-click Dial-Up Adapter.

Delete the Network Components You Don't Need

When you installed TCP/IP, you added some components that aren't needed for stand-alone Internet access. Go ahead and delete these components:

- Existing Ndis2 Driver
- IPX/SPX-compatible Protocol -> Dial-Up Adapter
- IPX/SPX-compatible Protocol -> Existing Ndis2 Driver
- NetBEUI -> Dial-Up Adapter
- NetBEUI > Existing Ndis2 Driver

To delete the unneeded network components:

1. In the Network dialog box, select (highlight) one of the above network components.
2. Select the Remove button.

In this lesson, you learned how to install Windows 95 TCP/IP. In the next lesson, you learn how to set up your Windows 95 SLIP/PPP connection.

CONFIGURING THE WINDOWS 95 PPP/SLIP CONNECTION

In this lesson, you learn how to set up your Windows 95 SLIP/PPP connection.

SETTING UP THE SLIP/PPP CONNECTION

In the last lesson, you completed the first step in configuring your Internet connection—installing the TCP/IP client. The next step is to configure the TCP/IP client and the SLIP/PPP connection.

Serial Line Internet Protocol (SLIP) and **Point-to-Point Protocol (PPP)** are two types of Internet accounts most users presently turn to. SLIP is the older of the two types of Internet connections explained here. As its name implies, SLIP allows you to connect to a service provider over a serial communication line, such as a telephone line. Developed after SLIP, PPP is also serial in nature, but it provides a higher degree of error detection and compression in its connection to your service provider. When given a choice, choose PPP.

1. If you aren't already in the Network dialog box, select the Start button on the taskbar and choose Settings, Control Panel. Double-click the Network icon.

2. In the Network dialog box, select Dial-Up Adapter. Select the Properties button to open the Dial-Up Adapter Properties sheet (see Figure 4.1).

Configuring the Windows 95 PPP/SLIP Connection 19

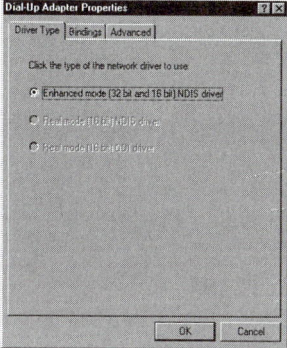

Figure 4.1 Dial-Up Adapter Properties sheet.

3. On the Driver Type page, select the Enhanced mode (32 bit and 16 bit) NDIS Driver radio button. The other two options may be grayed out because the enhanced mode driver is normally the default choice. On the Bindings page, select the TCP/IP check box. On the Advanced page, make sure **Record a log file** has the value No. Make sure **Use IPX header compression** has the value Yes. Choose OK to save your settings.

4. Select TCP/IP from the list of installed network components. Select the Properties button to open the TCP/IP Properties sheet (see Figure 4.2).

5. On the IP Address page, select the Obtain an IP address automatically radio button if you are a SLIP/PPP user who gets your IP address *dynamically* (if the IP address of your PC is set by you and remains the same, or if it is set for you by your provider when you log in, and thus can be different each time—ask your provider). If you're a static SLIP/PPP user, select the Specify an IP address radio button and enter the IP Address and the Subnet Mask in the appropriate fields (obtain from your provider).

20   LESSON 4

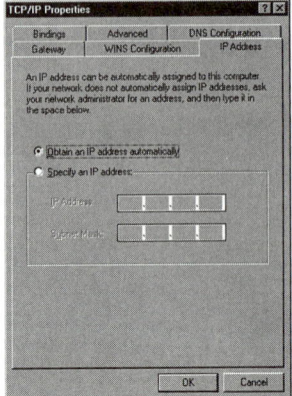

FIGURE 4.2   TCP/IP Properties sheet.

IP Address   An IP address is a four part numeric address (in the form *nnn.nnn.nnn.nnn*) assigned to all devices using the TCP/IP protocol, which includes all devices on the Internet. Because all devices have a unique number, or IP address, it is used to locate devices.

Subnet Mask   A subnet mask is an address, similar in form to an IP address (i.e., *nnn.nnn.nnn.nnn*) that is used to identify a portion of your providers network.

6. On the Gateway page, in the **New Gateway** field, enter the IP address of either your host provider (for a dynamic IP address user) or your own IP address (for a static IP address user). Again, your provider can provide this information.

7. On the Bindings page, select the Client for Microsoft Networks check box.

8. On the DNS Configuration page, select the Enable DNS (Domain Name Service) radio button. Enter your host IP address in the **Host** field and enter your host domain name in the **Domain** field. You have to get both of these from your provider. You also need to ask your provider if you have more than one DNS server to search. At the very least, enter the IP address of your host. Select the Add button after each entry.

9. Choose OK to save all your TCP/IP configuration settings and return to the Configuration tab of the Network dialog box.

10. Under Primary Network Logon, select Client for Microsoft Network. Select the Identification tab at the top of the dialog box (see Figure 4.3).

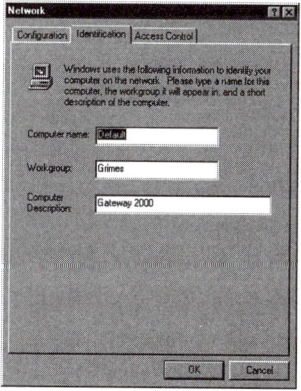

FIGURE 4.3 Identification tab of the Network dialog box.

11. You can enter almost anything you like here, but you need to place something in each field. If the fields already contain entries, you can accept or change them. Choose OK.

You should get a message informing you to insert your Windows 95 CD-ROM or your Windows 95 installation disks. Insert the CD or disks into the appropriate drive. When the needed files are copied, you will receive a message informing you that you need to restart Windows for the changes you just made to take effect. Choose OK to restart Windows.

In this lesson, you configured your SLIP or PPP connection. In the next lesson, you configure Windows 95 Dial-Up Networking.

LESSON 5

SETTING UP WINDOWS 95 WITH DIAL-UP NETWORKING

In this lesson, you learn how to set up your Internet connection with Windows Dial-Up Networking.

HOW TO SET UP DIAL-UP NETWORKING

This is the final step for configuring your Windows 95 Internet connection. In this lesson, you set up the Dial-Up Networking feature so that you can call your Internet Service Provider (ISP):

1. On the Windows 95 desktop, double-click the My Computer icon. In the My Computer window, the last item listed should be **Dial-Up Networking** (see Figure 5.1).

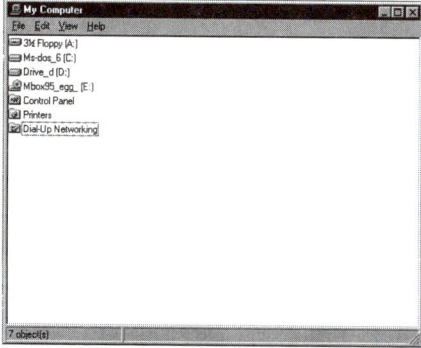

FIGURE 5.1 Dial-Up Networking listed in My Computer.

LESSON 5

Dial-Up Networking Isn't There! If Dial-Up Networking doesn't appear in the My Computer window, you probably didn't install it when you installed Windows 95. Open the Control Panel and select the Add/Remove Programs icon. In the Add/Remove Programs dialog box, select the Windows Setup tab. Highlight Communications and select the Details button. Select the Dial-Up Networking check box, and choose OK. Follow the prompts to complete the installation of Dial-Up Networking.

2. Double-click Dial-Up Networking to open the Dial-Up Networking dialog box. Double-click Make New Connection to open the Make New Connection dialog box (see Figure 5.2).

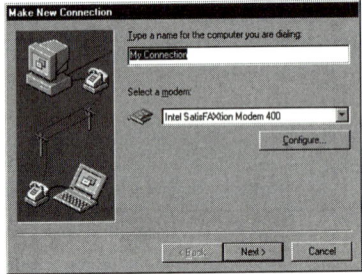

FIGURE 5.2 Make New Connection dialog box.

3. Enter a name for your connection in the **Type a name for the computer you are dialing** field. This is just a name or identifying label, so it can be anything you like.

4. If your modem is not selected in the **Select a modem** field, select the modem that you have installed in your PC. Select the Configure button to configure your modem according to the communications settings you plan to use for the General, Connection, and Options tabs. This brings up the properties sheet for your modem type.

Setting Up Windows 95 with Dial-Up Networking

> **My Modem Type Isn't There!** If by some remote chance Windows 95 can't configure your modem (it contains configuration information for hundreds of modems), you need to configure it using a configuration disk supplied by the manufacturer. Go to the Add New Hardware dialog box (in the Control Panel window, select the Add New Hardware icon) and follow the prompts. Another important point to consider is that if Windows 95 doesn't recognize your modem, the modem is probably too old, too slow, or too nonstandard to perform satisfactorily on the Internet.

5. Select the Options tab. Select Bring up terminal window after dialing. Choose OK to save modem configuration settings. This will close the modem properties sheet and allow you to continue in the Make New Connection dialog box.

6. Select the Next> button. If your area code is not entered correctly, enter your area code. In the **Telephone number** field, enter the number you dial to connect to your Internet provider. Make sure your country code is entered correctly (see Figure 5.3). If you use more than one provider, you will have to create a new connection for each one. You cannot leave the phone number blank (it won't let you) and enter a phone number at dial-up time.

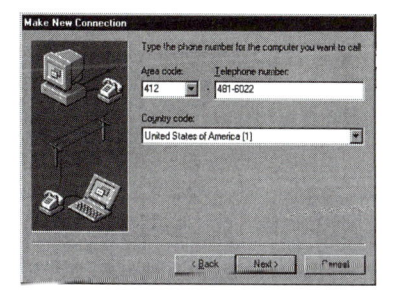

FIGURE 5.3 Entries for Make New Connection dialog box.

7. Select the Next> button. If you want to change the name you use for this connection, you can. Now select the Finish> button to complete the configuration for Dial-Up Networking.

In this lesson, you finished the configuration of your Internet connection by setting up your Dial-Up Networking connection. If you didn't purchase the Windows 95 add-on Microsoft Plus!, proceed to Lesson 7, "Using Dial-Up Networking To Get on the Internet."

LESSON 6
USING THE INTERNET SETUP WIZARD

In this lesson, you learn how to set up your Internet connection using the Internet Wizard in Microsoft Plus!.

INSTALLING MICROSOFT PLUS!

Microsoft Plus! is an add-on product for Windows 95 that gives you system- and disk-maintenance tools, desktop-enhancement products, Internet support, and a really cool pinball game. Before you can use the Internet Setup Wizard, you have to install Microsoft Plus!.

> **TIP** **For PPP Only** The Internet Setup Wizard only works for PPP (Point-to-Point Protocol) connections.

If you haven't installed Microsoft Plus!, go ahead and insert the CD or disk into the appropriate drive and follow the installation instructions. After you've installed it, look over Table 6.1, which lists the information you need to get from your provider so you can enter it when you run the Setup wizard.

TABLE 6.1 INFORMATION YOUR ISP SHOULD SUPPLY

INFORMATION	DEFINITION
Domain Server or IP Address	The provider's 12-digit IP address (*nnn.nnn.nnn.nnn*); each segment value is in the range 0-255.
Subnet Mask	Another 12-digit address in the form *nnn.nnn.nnn.nnn*.
Domain Name	Your provider's domain name, in the form *provider.com* or *provider.net*.
Host Name	If used (some providers tell you to leave this blank), your provider supplies it.
Mail Server Name	Your email server's domain name.
News Server Name	Your newsgroup server's domain name.
Email Address	Your email address in the form *username@mailserver*.
Commands used to log in to ISP	Commands such as "Enter user name and password" and any subsequent commands you need to follow to log in to the provider.
Whether IP address is dynamic or static	Your provider assigns the IP address if it's static.
Dial-Up phone number	The phone number you dial to connect to your provider.

USING THE INTERNET SETUP WIZARD   29

Running the Internet Setup Wizard

The Internet Setup Wizard is installed under the Internet Tools menu under Accessories. In this lesson, you will see step-by-step how to supply the information the Setup wizard needs to create your Internet connection. Remember, your use of the Internet Setup Wizard will differ if you use a different provider and connect from a different city.

To start the Internet Setup Wizard:

1. Select the Start button on the taskbar and choose Programs, Accessories, Internet Tools, and Internet Setup Wizard (see Figure 6.1).

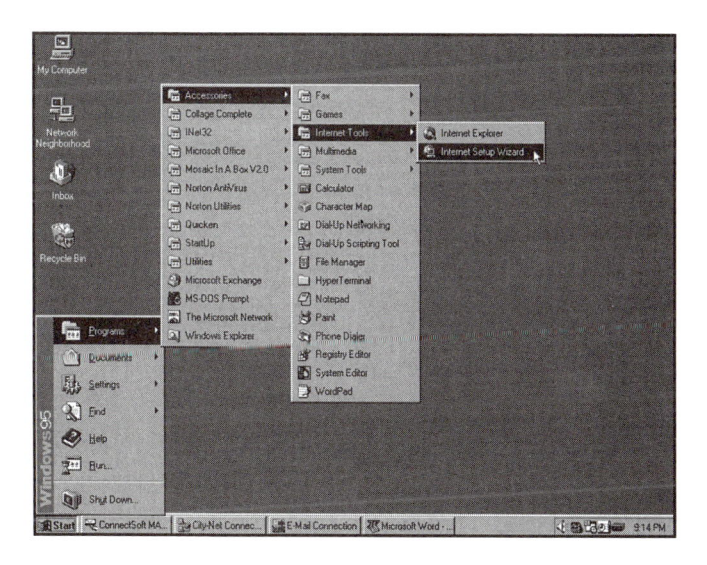

FIGURE 6.1 Menu path to Internet Setup Wizard.

2. At the opening screen, click the Next> button to begin.

3. In the How to Connect dialog box, select the I already have an account with a different service provider radio button (see Figure 6.2). Then select the Next> button.

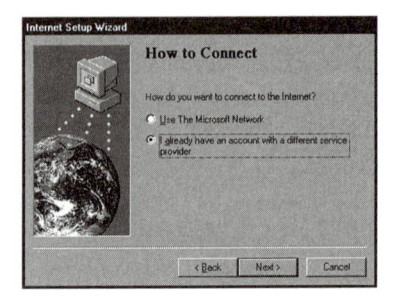

FIGURE 6.2 Installing Internet support with your own ISP.

4. In the Service Provider Information dialog box, enter a name for your Internet Service Provider (see Figure 6.3). This is just a label that identifies the shortcut icon you will use to connect to your provider. It can be anything you like. Select the Next> button to continue.

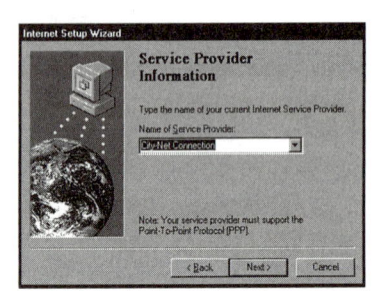

FIGURE 6.3 Supply a name for your provider.

5. In the Phone Number dialog box, enter the phone number of your provider. Even if you're dialing a local number, enter the area code and country code (select the correct code from the Country Code drop-down list). Finally, select the Bring up terminal window after dialing check box (see Figure 6.4). You will use the terminal window to log in to your ISP. Select the Next> button to continue.

USING THE INTERNET SETUP WIZARD   31

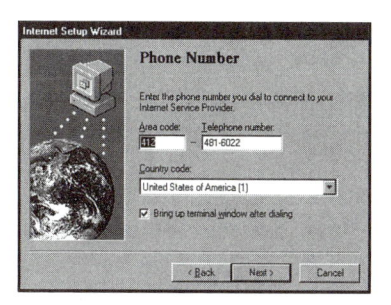

FIGURE 6.4   Supply your provider's phone number.

6. In the User Name and Password dialog box, enter the login name (user name) and password set up for you by your provider (see Figure 6.5). Even though you enter your user name and password here, some login systems by some providers will not accept these unless you also type them in the terminal window. Select the Next> button to continue.

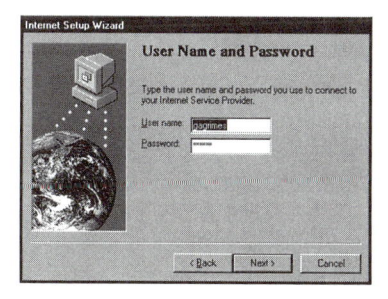

FIGURE 6.5   Supply your user name and password.

7. In the IP Address dialog box, select how you get your user IP address. Your provider should supply you with this information (see Figure 6.6). Select the Next> button to continue.

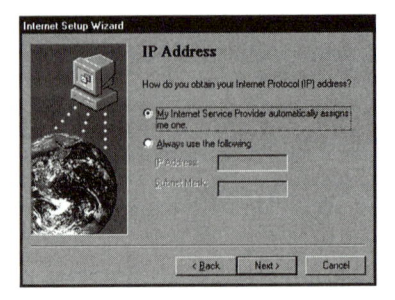

FIGURE 6.6 Supply your IP address information.

8. In the DNS Server Address dialog box, enter the IP address of your DNS (Domain Name Service) server. Your provider should supply you with this information (see Figure 6.7). If your provider also supplies you with an Alternate DNS server, enter that address in the second field. Select the Next> button to continue.

> **DNS (Domain Name Service)** DNS is just a means of converting the 12-digit IP address (*nnn.nnn.nnn.nnn*) into a recognizable name. For example, the provider I use in Pittsburgh has the IP address 199.234.118.2, which corresponds to the Domain name city-net.com.

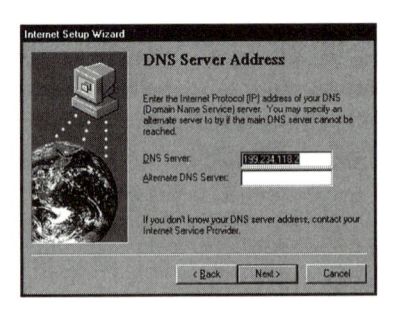

FIGURE 6.7 Supply the IP address of your DNS server.

9. In the Internet Mail dialog box, select the Use Internet Mail check box, and then enter your email address and the name of your mail server. Your provider should supply you with this information (see Figure 6.8). Select the Next> button to continue.

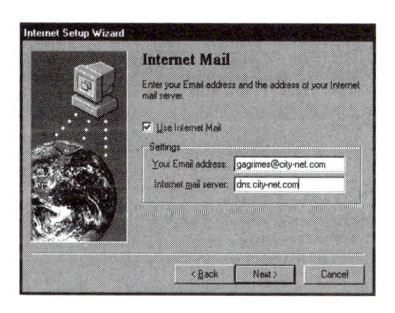

FIGURE 6.8   Supply your email information.

10. In the Exchange Profile dialog box, enter the Microsoft Exchange profile name to use for Internet mail. Use the name, **Internet Mail Setting**, as you see in Figure 6.9, which is the default profile name. Select the Next> button to continue.

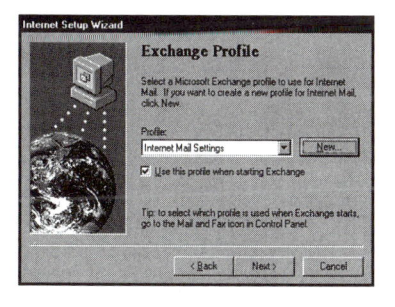

FIGURE 6.9   Set the MS Exchange profile name for Internet mail.

Lesson 6

11. Finally, select the Finish button to complete your wizard setup. When your Internet setup is complete, the Wizard will create an Internet icon on your desktop (see Figure 6.10). You can select this icon to connect to the Internet through your provider.

In this lesson, you learned how to use the Internet Setup Wizard in Microsoft Plus! to set up your Internet connection with your service provider. In the next lesson, you use your connection to sign on to the Internet.

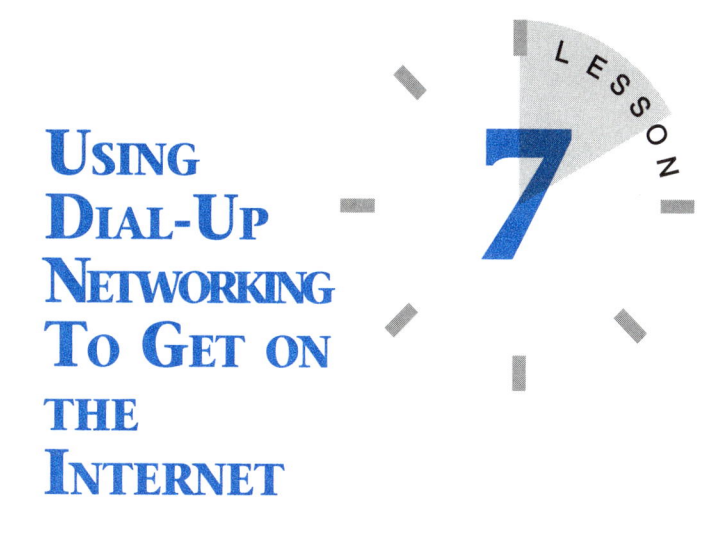

LESSON 7
Using Dial-Up Networking To Get on the Internet

In this lesson, you connect to the Internet with the Dial-Up Networking connection you created in the previous lessons.

Connecting to the Internet

In the previous lessons, you configured your Microsoft Networking client, installed and configured Microsoft TCP/IP, and configured the Dial-Up Networking client for your Internet provider. Now it's time to test your work.

Bear in mind that what you enter to connect to your provider might be different from what you see in this lesson. The figures in this lesson show my connection to my Internet provider using a Point-to-Point Protocol (PPP) connection over a 14.4 modem. Your provider should have given you the necessary information for you to log in, such as when to enter your login name (or ID) and your password, and any additional information required.

> **TIP** **Check the Info from Your ISP** To double-check the information you got from your Internet provider, compare it to the list in Table 6.1 of Lesson 6. It's possible your ISP provided you with more information than is listed in the table, but you should not have received less.

What you see here should be enough additional information to help you connect to the Internet.

1. Double-click the Internet icon located on your desktop. This starts the Microsoft Internet Explorer browser (if you purchased and installed Microsoft Plus!). The Connect To dialog box appears (see Figure 7.1).

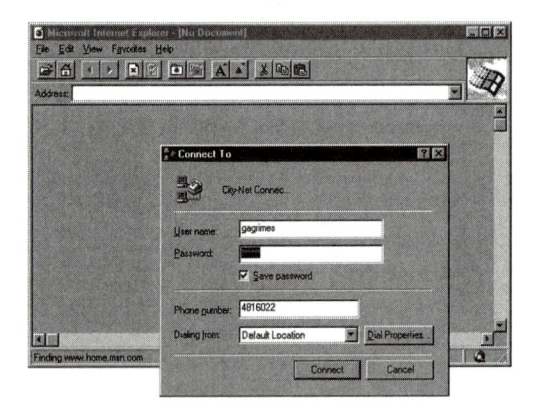

FIGURE 7.1 Connecting to your provider with MS Internet Explorer.

If you didn't purchase Microsoft Plus!, double-click the My Computer desktop icon and then double-click the Dial-Up Networking icon. In the Dial-Up Networking dialog box, double-click the connection you created with your provider. With or without Microsoft Plus!, you should now see the connection you created with your provider, with the information you supplied for your login name, password, and provider's phone number.

2. In the Connect To dialog box, select the Connect button to dial your provider (see Figure 7.2).

FIGURE 7.2   Dialing your provider.

> **My Connection Setup Didn't Dial!**   If your connection setup didn't dial, your modem might not be installed correctly. Check the manual supplied by your modem manufacturer, and check the Modems configuration utility in the Control Panel.

3. If you connect to your provider, the Post-Dial Terminal Screen window now appears and prompts you to enter the information supplied by your provider (see Figure 7.3). Enter the information (login name, password, and so on). When done, select the Continue button or press the F7 key.

> **TIP**
>
> **Script Your Login!**   Instead of having to type and re-type your login commands each time you connect to your provider, why not create a script to do it? If you purchased Microsoft Plus!, look in the Plus! folder for the file SCRIPT.DOC. It details how to create an automated dial-up script.

4. If your connection settings are correct and you enter the correct information required by your provider, in a few seconds, a message indicates that you are connected (see Figure 7.4). Notice that the connection keeps a clock running that shows you how long you are connected and the speed of your connection. You may find it convenient now to close My Computer and Dial-Up Networking.

Do *not* close the Connect To program; minimize it instead. If you close it, you exit the program and break the connection you just established.

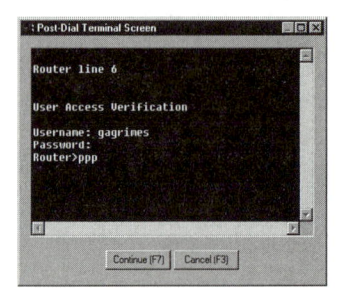

FIGURE 7.3 Post-Dial Terminal Screen window.

FIGURE 7.4 Connection completed.

Before continuing, test your connection with a testing utility supplied with Windows 95—WinIPCfg.

1. Select the Start button on the taskbar and choose Programs MS-DOS Prompt to open a DOS window.

2. Type winipcfg and press Enter to run the WinIPCfg utility program. In a few seconds, the IP information you see in Figure 7.5 appears. Select the More Info>> button to display Figure 7.6.

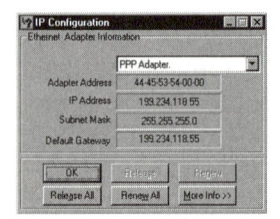

FIGURE 7.5 WinIPCfg displaying IP information.

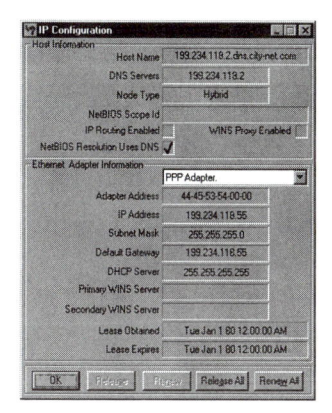

FIGURE 7.6 More information from WinIPCfg.

Most of the information displayed by WinIPCfg probably doesn't mean much to you, but the information should indicate whether you're connected to your provider, such as your provider's name and IP address in the **Host Name** field. The information in the **IP Address** field should be either your static IP address (if you set your own) or the dynamic IP address supplied by your provider (if you didn't notice, back in the Post-Dial Terminal Screen window, your IP address was displayed).

> **Is WinIPCfg Working?** To make sure WinIPCfg isn't supplying you with false information, try running WinIPCfg before you connect to your provider. WinIPCfg should display your IP address as **0.0.0.0**, which means you aren't connected.

In this lesson, you learned how to connect to your provider using the connection you created in Windows 95, and how to test your connection. In the next lesson, you learn how to use the Internet utility FTP (File Transfer Protocol) to download files.

LESSON 8
USING THE WINDOWS 95 FTP UTILITY

In this lesson, you learn how to use the Windows 95 FTP file downloading utility.

WHAT IS THE WINDOWS 95 FTP?

Windows 95 includes a few Internet utilities, one of which is **FTP**. FTP, short for File Transfer Protocol, is a very useful program that allows you to transfer all types of files from an Internet computer, called an **FTP server**, to your PC. The only problem, which you will see firsthand, is that the FTP utility that's included with Windows 95 is a DOS, text-based utility that's a bit cumbersome to use. Fortunately, you will only need to use it in this lesson. Afterward, you will never have to use it again because, in this lesson, you will use it to download a Windows-based FTP utility that's a lot easier to use.

> **Download** Download is an old mainframe computer term that simply means to copy a file or program from a host computer "down" to your computer. And as you might have guessed, the opposite of **download** is **upload**, which means to copy a file from your computer "up" to the host computer.

> **Virus Alert!** Be aware that when you access an FTP server, you are potentially exposing your computer to computer viruses. Most server administrators scan all files that come into their servers, but occasionally some infected files do get in. Always make sure you run an up-to-date anti-virus program before you download files. Also, make sure the anti-virus programs (some experts recommend using more than one) you use are specifically made for Windows 95. Anti-virus programs not made to work with Windows 95 might appear to be operating correctly, but they are not! Two programs that consistently get good reviews are Norton Anti-Virus and McAfee.

Using FTP

To use the Windows 95 FTP utility, first make sure that you are connected to your Internet provider:

1. Select the Start button on the taskbar and choose Programs, MS-DOS Prompt. You can just as easily start the FTP utility using the Run command, but because it's a DOS-based program, I prefer to start it in a DOS window.

2. At the DOS prompt, type **ftp** and press Enter. This starts FTP and gives you FTP's prompt (see Figure 8.1).

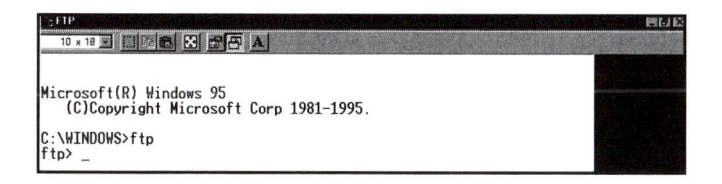

```
Microsoft(R) Windows 95
    (C)Copyright Microsoft Corp 1981-1995.
C:\WINDOWS>ftp
ftp> _
```

FIGURE 8.1 Windows 95 FTP utility.

3. For this lesson, you're going to log in to the FTP server gatekeeper.dec.com and download the file ws_ftp32.zip. To log in to gatekeeper.dec.com, type the command open

ftpserver, where *ftpserver* is the name of the FTP server to which you want to log in (see Figure 8.2).

> **TIP**
>
> **Got a Copy of PKUNZIP?** Many files you find on FTP servers will have the file extension ZIP. This means that they are compressed file archives. To decompress files of this type, you need a program called PKUNZIP. If you don't have a copy of PKUNZIP, you can download a copy at **gatekeeper.dec.com**. The file to download is pk206g.exe. Lesson 12 shows you how to download a Windows-based version of PKUNZIP, WinZip.

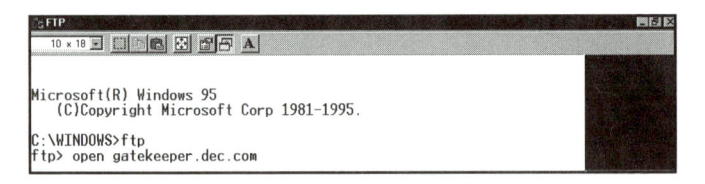

```
Microsoft(R) Windows 95
    (C)Copyright Microsoft Corp 1981-1995.
C:\WINDOWS>ftp
ftp> open gatekeeper.dec.com
```

FIGURE 8.2 Log in to gatekeeper.dec.com.

> **I Can't Log In!** FTP servers often have limits on the number of users who can log in at one time. When that limit is reached—which often happens on very popular servers—it will not permit any additional logins. If you get an error message similar to this, don't worry. Just try again later.

4. The FTP server will respond with the prompt **User (gatekeeper.dec.com:(none)):.** To log in, type the user name **anonymous**. Now, you're prompted to enter a password. Enter your email address as your password, and the FTP server grants you access (see Figure 8.3).

Using the Windows 95 FTP Utility   43

```
 FTP
 10 x 18
         Extended commands available via:
            quote site exec COMMAND
         Where COMMAND is one of:
            index PATTERN   - to glance through our index (uses agrep).  example:
                              ftp> quote site exec index emacs

         This FTP server is based on the 4.3BSD-Reno version.  Our modified sources
         are in /pub/DEC/gwtools.

         If you are connecting to gatekeeper from a VMS system running a version of
         UCX earlier than V2.0, a bug in UCX will prevent the automatic login from
         working. To get around this, wait for the message that says:
            %UCX-E-FTP_LOGREJ, Login request rejected
         and then log in by hand with the "login" command at the "FTP>" prompt.  You

         should also consider upgrading to the latest version of UCX.

220 gatekeeper.dec.com FTP server (Version 5.181 Fri Jun 16 12:01:35 PDT 1995) r
eady.
User (gatekeeper.dec.com:(none)): anonymous ─────────┐
331 Guest login ok, send ident as password.
Password:                                                     │
230 Guest login ok, access restrictions apply.                │
ftp>
```
└ Enter password   Login anonymous   Log in as
  (not displayed)   accepted   "anonymous"

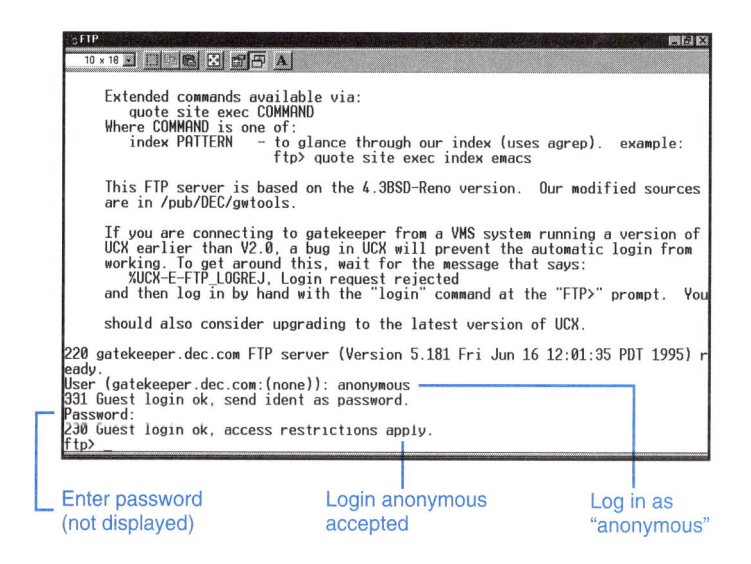

Figure 8.3 Access granted to gatekeeper.dec.com.

5. The file that you want is in the /pub/micro/msdos/
   win3/winsock directory. To change to that directory, issue
   the change directory command **cd *directory***, where directory is the full directory path; for this example, the
   command is:

   cd pub/micro/msdos/win3/winsock

   This command takes you to the designated directory (see
   Figure 8.4).

6. To download program files, enter the **binary** command
   before you begin the file download. This instructs the FTP
   server to prepare to do a binary (non-text) file download.
   Then enter the **get *filename drive:\newfilename*** command to download (get) the file you want (*filename*) to
   the drive with the file name you designate (*newfilename*).
   For this example, the complete command is:

   get ws_ftp32.zip c:\ws_ftp32.zip

   This command downloads the file ws_ftp32.zip to your
   C:\ drive (see Figure 8.5).

Lesson 8

```
quote site exec COMMAND
Where COMMAND is one of:
    index PATTERN    - to glance through our index (uses agrep).  example:
                        ftp> quote site exec index emacs

This FTP server is based on the 4.3BSD-Reno version.  Our modified sources
are in /pub/DEC/gwtools.

If you are connecting to gatekeeper from a VMS system running a version of
UCX earlier than V2.0, a bug in UCX will prevent the automatic login from
working.  To get around this, wait for the message that says:
    %UCX-E-FTP_LOGREJ, Login request rejected
and then log in by hand with the "login" command at the "FTP>" prompt.  You
should also consider upgrading to the latest version of UCX.

220 gatekeeper.dec.com FTP server (Version 5.181 Fri Jun 16 12:01:35 PDT 1995) r
eady.
User (gatekeeper.dec.com:(none)): anonymous
331 Guest login ok, send ident as password.
Password:
230 Guest login ok, access restrictions apply.
ftp> cd pub/micro/msdos/win3/winsock
250 CWD command successful.
ftp>
```

— cd command to desired directory

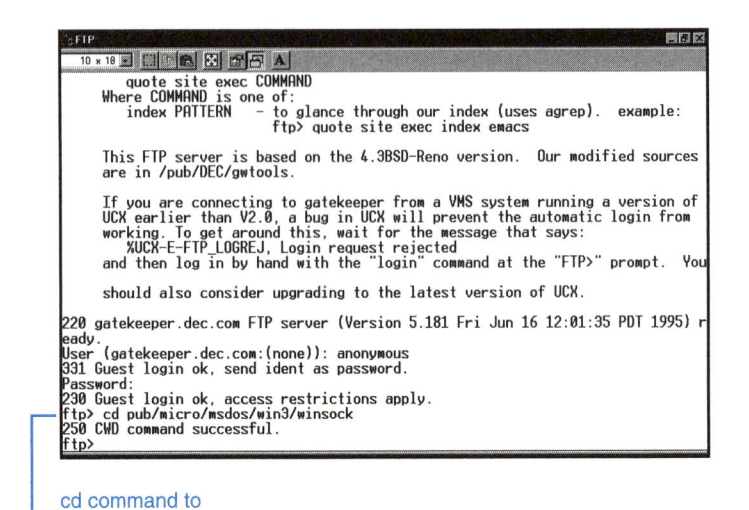

FIGURE 8.4 Changing directories in the FTP server.

```
This FTP server is based on the 4.3BSD-Reno version.  Our modified sources
are in /pub/DEC/gwtools.

If you are connecting to gatekeeper from a VMS system running a version of
UCX earlier than V2.0, a bug in UCX will prevent the automatic login from
working.  To get around this, wait for the message that says:
    %UCX-E-FTP_LOGREJ, Login request rejected
and then log in by hand with the "login" command at the "FTP>" prompt.  You
should also consider upgrading to the latest version of UCX.

220 gatekeeper.dec.com FTP server (Version 5.181 Fri Jun 16 12:01:35 PDT 1995) r
eady.
User (gatekeeper.dec.com:(none)): anonymous
331 Guest login ok, send ident as password.
Password:
230 Guest login ok, access restrictions apply.
ftp> cd pub/micro/msdos/win3/winsock
250 CWD command successful.
ftp> binary
200 Type set to I.
ftp> get ws_ftp32.zip c:\ws_ftp32.zip
200 PORT command successful.
150 Opening BINARY mode data connection for ws_ftp32.zip (152695 bytes).
```

— Binary command   Get command

FIGURE 8.5 Download ws_ftp32.zip.

When the file is done downloading, the FTP server will indicate that the download is finished, how long it took, and the speed of the download.

7. To log out of the FTP server, type the **quit** command.

   This command logs you out and takes you back to the DOS prompt. To return to Windows, enter the **exit** command.

In this lesson, you learned how to download files using the Windows 95 FTP utility. In the next lesson, you learn how to use the Windows based FTP utility that you downloaded in this lesson.

LESSON 9

USING A WINDOWS-BASED FTP UTILITY—WS_FTP32

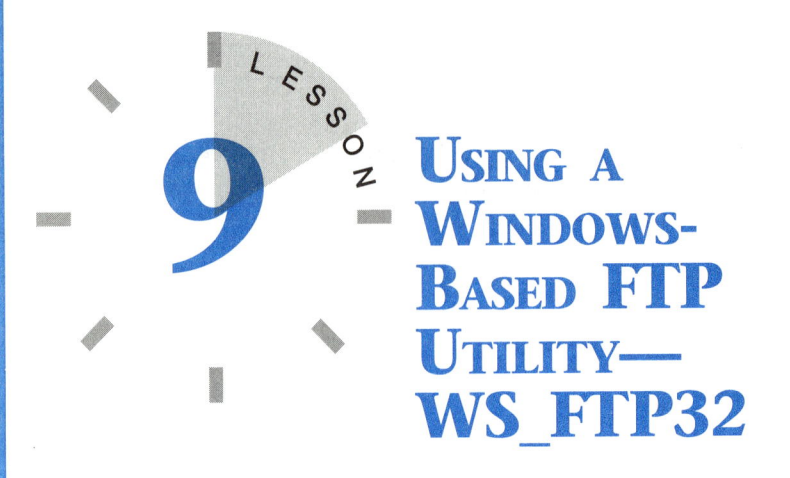

In this lesson, you learn how to use the Windows-based FTP utility WS_FTP32.

INSTALLING WS_FTP32

In the last lesson, you learned how to use the Windows 95 utility, FTP, to download a file from an FTP server. FTP is as capable as any other FTP utility program, as you experienced in the last lesson, but it's somewhat awkward to use; you must remember the commands to enter for each operation you want to perform.

The FTP utility featured in this lesson is a lot easier to use. It's a Windows-based application, so most of its operation involves pointing and clicking.

The file you downloaded, ws_ftp32.zip, is in a compressed archive format, so, as you also learned in the last lesson, you need a program to decompress it, such as PKUNZIP. To decompress ws_ftp32.zip, copy both (pkunzip.exe and ws_ftp32.zip) into a folder, open a DOS window, and type:

> **pkunzip ws_ftp32**

When ws_ftp32.zip finishes decompressing, install it as you would any other application in Windows 95. If you're not sure how to install an application in Windows 95, consult your Windows 95 documentation or Help system.

Using a Windows-Based FTP Utility—WS_FTP32 47

Running WS_FTP32

Now that you've gotten WS_FTP32 installed, you're ready to start using WS_FTP32 as your FTP utility:

1. Select the Start button on the taskbar and choose Program, WS_FTP32 (created when you installed it). Now you can use WS_FTP32 to download some additional files that you will use in some of the later lessons. The Session Profile dialog box should now appear.

2. If the Session Profile dialog box doesn't appear automatically, select the Connect button. In the Session Profile window, select the New button, and the Session Profile dialog box clears, ready for you to enter a new profile. You can now enter the information for the FTP server you're going to log in to (see Figure 9.1).

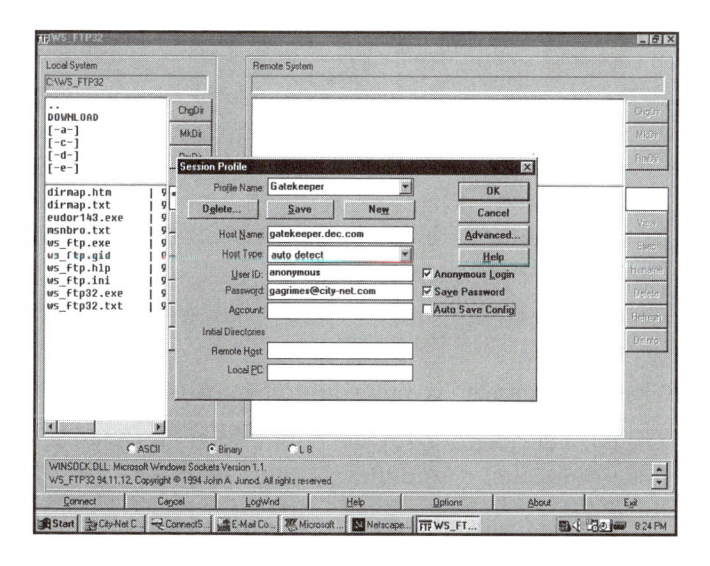

Figure 9.1   Session Profile window of WS_FTP32.

3. Select Gatekeeper from the **Profile Name** drop-down list. In the **Host Name** field, enter **gatekeeper.dec.com**. In the **User ID** field, enter

Anonymous, or check the Anonymous Login check box. In the **Password** field, enter your email address in the form *userid@provider-server* (in my case, I would enter gagrimes@city-net.com). Select the Save Password check box. To save the information you entered, select the Save button.

> **TIP** **Type Your Address Once** If you select the Options button from the toolbar at the bottom of the screen, the Options dialog box appears. You then can select the Program Options button; you only have to enter your email address once. Then you simply have to select the Anonymous Login check box to enter your password. Just close the Session Profile dialog box first.

4. Choose OK to log in to Gatekeeper.

> **I Couldn't Log In!** FTP servers often have limits regarding the number of users who can log in at one time. When that limit is reached—which often happens on very popular servers—it will not permit any additional logins. If you get an error message saying your login attempt failed, don't panic. Just try again later.

WS_FTP32's main screen is divided into two parts:

- The left side, identified as the **Local System**, shows the folders (directories) and files on your computer.

- The right side, identified as the **Remote System**, shows the folders (directories) and files on the computer you've logged in to.

Notice that each side is divided into an upper and lower portion or window. The upper portion shows the folders (directories)

Using a Windows-Based FTP Utility—WS_FTP32

available to you on that drive or FTP server. The lower portion shows the files that are stored in the folder you are accessing. When more folders or files exist than fit in each portion, a scroll bar appears. Use it to navigate the list.

There are two arrows in the bar separating the Local System window from the Remote System window. One arrow points to the left and one arrow points to the right. Use these arrows to move files between the Remote and Local systems. To move a file from the Remote System to the Local System, highlight the file and then click the arrow pointing to the left. To move a file from the Local System to the Remote System, use the arrow pointing to the right. You also can select multiple files to download or upload using the Shift or Ctrl keys just as you would with any Windows file list.

The file you want to download in this lesson is eudor143.zip, which is located in the pub/micro/msdos/win3/winsock directory. It is a popular shareware email program called Eudora. You can use this file in Lesson 10, "Sending Email with Microsoft Exchange."

1. In the upper window of the Remote System, scroll down until you see the folder (directory) pub and double-click it. Continue this procedure through folders micro, msdos, win3, and winsock until you are in folder winsock.

2. Scroll down through the lower window on the Remote System until you locate the file eudor143.zip. Click eudor143.zip once to highlight it.

3. Click the left arrow to download eudor143.zip from Gatekeeper to your PC. In Figure 9.2, you see the Transfer Status window showing the status of your file transfer. Depending on the size of the file and the speed of your Internet connection, the file can take anywhere from a few seconds to a few minutes to download. When you complete the download, WS_FTP32 stores the file in the folder that you last accessed on your Local System—which, by default, is the folder where the WS_FTP32 application program is stored.

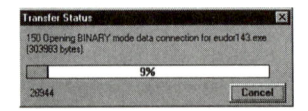

FIGURE 9.2 A file being downloaded.

If you noticed the three radio buttons near the bottom of the screen (ASCII, Binary, L8). They are used to set the transfer mode type. Binary is set by default, and for most transfers you can leave it set to the Binary default. If you know the file you're transferring is purely text, you can use the ASCII mode. For more information on transfer mode, see "Transferring Files" in the Help section.

> **TIP**
>
> **Keep Your Files Together!** You'll find it convenient to create a folder within the folder where WS_FTP32 is stored, and use it to keep all of the files you download together. This helps keep your WS_FTP32 folder less cluttered.

4. When you finish downloading files, select the Exit button to log out of the FTP server and to exit WS_FTP32.

In this lesson, you learned how to use the Windows-based program WS_FTP32 to download files from an FTP server. In the next lesson, you learn how to configure MS Exchange to send and receive email over the Internet.

LESSON 10

SENDING EMAIL WITH MICROSOFT EXCHANGE

In this lesson, you learn how to use MS Exchange to send and receive email over the Internet.

CONFIGURING MS EXCHANGE

When you configured your connection to your Internet Service Provider back in Lessons 3, 4, and 5 (or Lesson 6) you also installed MS Exchange. During this installation, you also did most of the configuration needed to run MS Exchange. The only configuration option you still need to perform is entering your password for your provider's mail server:

1. Select the Start button on the taskbar and choose Programs, MS Exchange to start MS Exchange (see Figure 10.1).

2. In the MS Exchange main window, select Tools, Options to open the Options dialog box. Then select the Services tab. Highlight Internet Mail, and then select the Properties button to open the Properties sheet (see Figure 10.2).

3. Enter your login password in the **Password** field. Choose OK. You return to the Options dialog box. Choose OK.

4. Exit MS Exchange and restart the program to activate the changes you just made.

52 LESSON 10

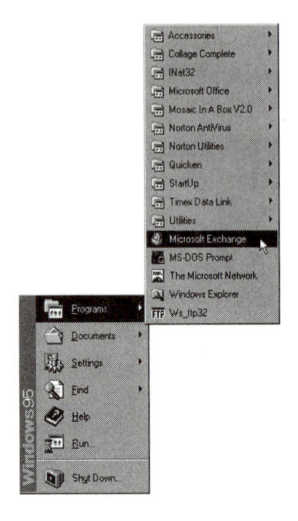

FIGURE 10.1 MS Exchange in your Windows 95 setup.

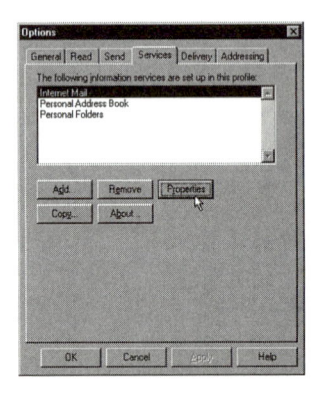

FIGURE 10.2 Selecting Internet Mail Properties.

KEEPING TRACK WITH YOUR ADDRESS BOOK

Before you start sending mail, you need to take care of one small housekeeping chore—setting up your Address Book. The Address

Book contains the names and email addresses of people to whom you regularly send email.

> **TIP** — **Address Books Save Time** You'll save yourself some time if you enter the names and email addresses of people you send mail to, especially if you regularly correspond with them. If these names and addresses are not in your Address Book, you have to manually type the names and addresses each time you want to send email.

To enter names into your personal Address Book:

1. From the MS Exchange menu, choose Tools, Address Book to open the Address Book dialog box (see Figure 10.3).

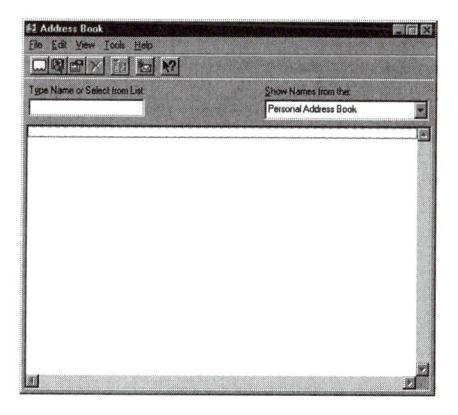

FIGURE 10.3 Address Book dialog box.

2. Open the File menu and choose New Entry. In the New Entry window, make sure that Internet Mail Address is highlighted and then choose OK. This sequence brings up the New Internet Mail Address Properties sheet.

3. In the **Display Name** field, enter the name of the person whose address you are entering. You can enter it either in the form *Bill Clinton* or *Clinton, Bill*. In the **Email Address** field, enter the person's email address in the form *bclinton@whitehouse.gov* (see Figure 10.4).

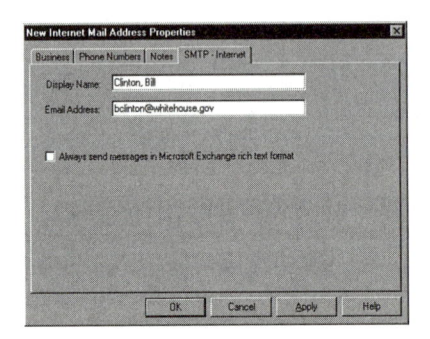

FIGURE 10.4 New Internet Mail Address Properties sheet showing address entry.

If you know for certain that this person is using MS Exchange as his email program, select the check box labeled **Always send messages in Microsoft Exchange rich text format**. If you're not sure, leave this box blank.

This information is all you're required to enter for each person in your Address Book. You can, however, enter additional (optional) information by selecting the tabs marked **Business**, **Phone Numbers**, and **Notes**. When you have entered all of the information for a person, choose OK to save the entry in your Address Book.

Type in as many entries as you want. When you finish, close the Address Book and return to the MS Exchange window.

CREATING AND SENDING EMAIL

The main purpose of any email application is to send email, so let's jump right in and send our first email message.

Sending Email with Microsoft Exchange 55

1. From the MS Exchange menu, choose Compose, New Message. This procedure opens the New Message dialog box where you can start to compose your email message.

2. In the **To** field, you can either type the email address of the person to whom you are sending the message, or select the To button to bring up your Address Book. In the Address Book, select the name from the displayed list of names and then select the To-> button. If you want to cc this message to someone, select the person's name and then select the CC-> button. Choose OK to return to the New Message window.

> **CC** CC, or Carbon Copy as it's known in the physical world, produces the same results here. A copy of the email message is sent to the user(s) listed in the cc section.

3. Enter a subject (optional). Click in the message window and type your message (see Figure 10.5).

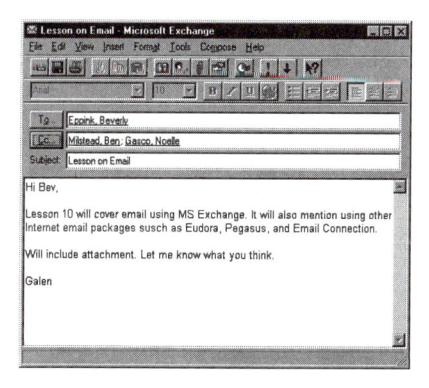

FIGURE 10.5 Sample email message.

4. When you have completed your message, you can send it by selecting the **Send** icon. It's the icon on the toolbar that looks like an envelope.

> **TIP** — **What Does Each Icon Do?** To see what each icon is used for, you can either open the Help section, or you can simply place the cursor on each icon and in one to two seconds a label appears describing the function of that particular icon.

Receiving Email

After you start sending out email, it won't be long before someone responds to one of your messages. To check to see if you have messages waiting:

> **TIP** — **Strangely Labeled Command!** To check email on your mail server, select Tools, Deliver Now. Normally you would expect something labeled **Deliver Now** to mean that you're delivering something to someone, but here it means that your email is being delivered to you. Strange, but true.

1. From the MS Exchange menu, choose Tools, Deliver Now. MS Exchange then logs in to your service provider's mail server and checks to see if your account has received any messages. If you have any messages waiting, MS Exchange notifies you (see Figure 10.6).

2. Select the Yes button. MS Exchange places your messages in your Inbox under Personal Folders.

3. To read a message in your Inbox, double-click the message. It opens in its own window (see Figure 10.7).

Sending Email with Microsoft Exchange

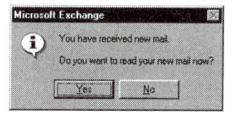

FIGURE 10.6 Email notification.

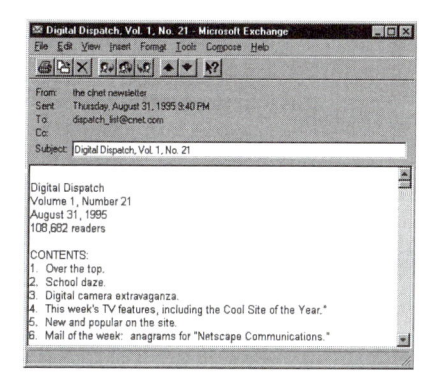

FIGURE 10.7 Reading a newly received email message.

EMOTICONS

Email has become so widespread that many users have taken to trying to add a new dimension to it. One of the problems often sited with email, which is usually straight text with no formatting or the ability to add emphasis, is that you lose the ability to add any feeling to your text. You (usually) can't add underlining, boldface, or italics, in attempt to add some expression of feeling. To overcome this limitation, some users have started adding what have come to be known as **emoticons** (emotional icons). You've probably seen them. They looked like smiley faces turned sideways. The following minitable shows some common emoticons and their meanings.

Emoticon	Meaning
:) or :-)	happy
:(	sad
:-<	mad
:-0	wow! or surprise
:-@	yelling
:-}	grin
;-)	wink

The only universally given advice on using emoticons is to do so sparingly.

Other Internet Email Programs

Obviously, this lesson can't cover all aspects of every option in MS Exchange. As an Internet email program, MS Exchange is somewhat top-heavy with "bells and whistles," which can overwhelm some users who might perceive the inclusion of all these options as overkill. If MS Exchange embodies all that you think a good email package should be, you might consider the Que title *Using Internet Explorer*, which has an excellent section on using Microsoft Exchange.

You can, however, choose a different Internet email program if you want. In Lesson 9, you downloaded one such program, Eudora, from the Gatekeeper FTP server. Try this popular email program and decide which program best suits your needs.

Two other popular email programs you can try are Pegasus and Email Connection. You can download Pegasus from **ftp://risc.ua.edu**.

The program file, WINPM201.ZIP, is located in the /pub/network/pegasus directory. You can download Email Connection from **ftp://emc.connectsoft.com**.

The program file, EMCSETUP.EXE, is located in the /pub/emc25/ emcsetup.exe directory.

Each program comes with a complete set of instructions and help files. Using what you have learned in this lesson, you should have no trouble installing and running any of them.

In this lesson, you learned how to use MS Exchange as your Internet email program. In the next lesson, you learn about the World Wide Web—undoubtedly the most popular part of the Internet.

LESSON 11 — DISCOVERING THE WORLD WIDE WEB

In this lesson, you discover the World Wide Web and find out why it's so popular.

WHAT IS THE WORLD WIDE WEB?

The World Wide Web is largely responsible for the current success and popularity of the Internet. One way to describe the World Wide Web, or just "the Web" for short, is to say that it is the multimedia section of the Internet. The Web gives you pictures and sounds, along with an almost infinite array of textual information.

I could easily spend the remainder of this lesson telling you what the Web is and what it has to offer, but because the Web is meant to be viewed and not talked about, perhaps the best way for you to learn about it is to experience it. To do this, you need a Web browser. A **Web browser** is a special type of program that allows you to view the text and pictures contained in Web screens or, as they are called on the Web, **Web pages**.

NETSCAPE NAVIGATOR

One of the most popular Web browsers is Netscape Navigator, or Netscape for short. You can get a copy of Netscape by using the FTP utility WS_FTP32, covered in Lesson 9. To download Netscape:

1. Start WS_FTP32 and create a new Session Profile for the Netscape FTP server by selecting the New button in the Session Profile dialog box.

2. Type **ftp.netscape.com** in the **Host name** field. Type **auto-detect** in the **Host Type** field. In the **User ID** field, type anonymous. In the **Password** field, type your email address. Select the Save button to save the information you just entered.

3. Choose OK to log in to the Netscape FTP server.

4. Once you log in to the Netscape FTP server, go to the /netscape/windows directory (folder) and download the N32E12N.EXE file. You'll notice that there is also a version on this FTP server called N16E12N.EXE. This is the 16-bit version used with Windows 3.1. The file N32E12N.EXE contains the 32-bit version used with Windows 95.

5. The file you just downloaded, N32E12N.EXE, is in an archival (compressed) format, like a ZIP file. The only difference is that it is a self-extracting, or self-decompressing file. To extract or decompress its contents, copy it into a folder by itself and run it the same as you would any other EXE program.

6. Once N32E12N.EXE is decompressed, use the Add/Remove Programs Wizard under Control Panel to install it the same as you would any other Windows program. After the installation you will have a Netscape icon inside a Netscape menu.

> **TIP**
>
> **I Have a Browser** If you already have a Web browser you're using, you can probably use your current browser to get a copy of Netscape. Point your browser to: **http://www.netscape.com** and follow the links to download the Netscape browser. A word of warning: This site is busy; the file will take 15-20 minutes at 14.4.

Discovering the Web

Now that you've installed Netscape, it's time to use it to start exploring the Web. This lesson doesn't teach you all the ins and outs of using Netscape, but it does teach you enough of the basics of Netscape to get you started exploring the Web.

To get to a site or page on the Web, you must tell your browser how to find that page. You learned in Lesson 8 that the Internet has devices called **FTP servers** that store files that you can download. The Internet also has devices called **Web servers**. These are servers that store the Web pages that your browser displays. One way to quickly and easily tell the difference between a Web server and an FTP server is by looking at the first few letters of the name. Web servers all begin with "http" and FTP servers all begin with "ftp."

1. Double-click the Netscape icon (in the Netscape menu) to start the program. The first thing you see is the license agreement, and then Netscape's colorful Web page or, more precisely, its home page (see Figure 11.1).

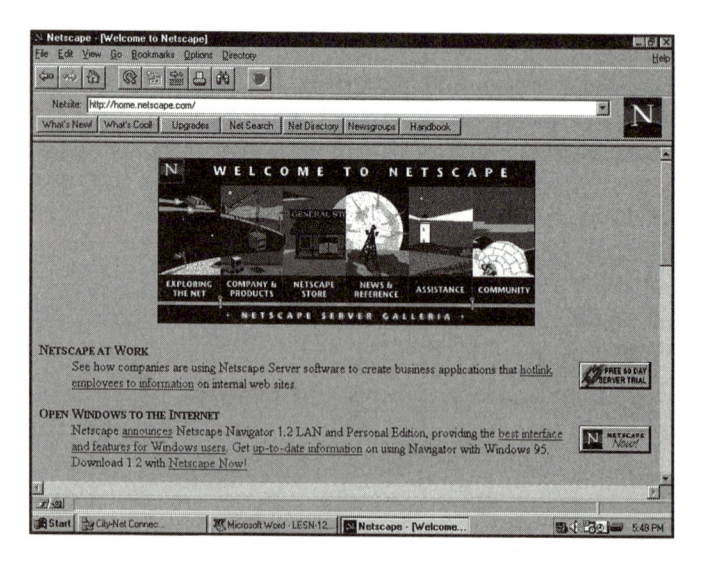

Figure 11.1 Netscape's home page.

Discovering the World Wide Web 63

> **Home Page** A home page is the name given to the opening screen or first page of a Web site belonging to a company, group, or organization on the World Wide Web. It is analogous to a welcome screen.

> **TIP**
> **Loading Web Pages Faster** Netscape is set to load all graphic files and images (pictures) with the text they accompany. On fast Internet connections, this is usually not a problem, but if you have a slow connection, you will often find yourself waiting for the pictures to load and display. To speed up page loading and display, select the Options menu and remove the checkmark from in front of Auto-Load Images. This procedure prevents the graphic files from loading automatically and instead places a small icon in its place. If you still want to view the image, click the Reload icon on the toolbar, and the image will then download and be displayed.

2. Before proceeding, stop and take a look at the nine icons underneath the menu. These nine icons make up the toolbar. The following minitable explains each icon's function.

Icon	Name	Description
	Back	Moves back to previously displayed page
	Forward	Moves forward to previously displayed page
	Home	Displays the home page
	Reload	Reloads an image being downloaded

Lesson 11

Icon	Name	Description
	Images	Displays images onto current page if they were not loaded automatically
	Open	Opens the Open Location dialog box in which you enter a new URL
	Print	Prints the currently displayed page
	Find	Finds text in the current page
	Stop	Stops the transfer of the current Web page

3. To go (the proper term is **jump**) to a different Web page, on the Netscape menu, choose File, Open Location. The Open Location dialog box appears (see Figure 11.2). Enter the following URL:

   http://www.paramount.com

   This procedure takes you to the Paramount Pictures home page (see Figure 11.3).

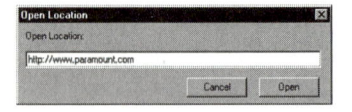

Figure 11.2 Netscape's Open Location dialog box.

> **TIP** **Entering URLs Quickly** You can also enter a URL in the location box just under the toolbar. Use the cursor to delete the contents of the location box, enter the URL you want to jump to, and press Enter.

DISCOVERING THE WORLD WIDE WEB

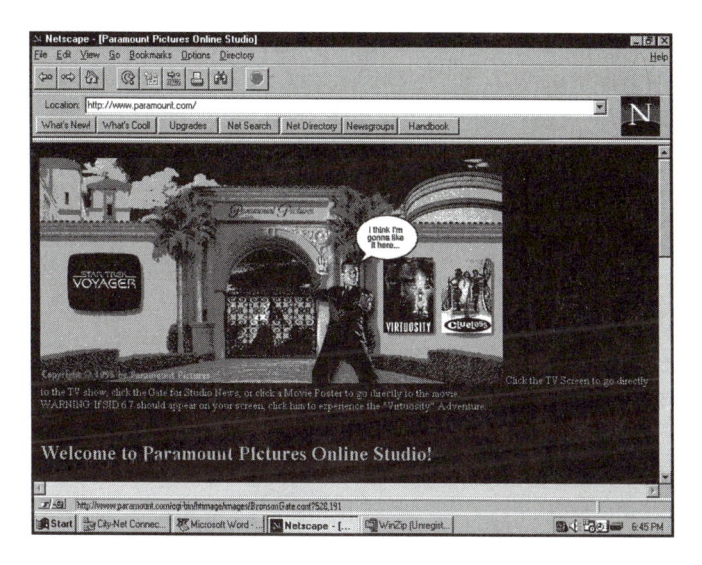

FIGURE 11.3 Paramount Pictures home page.

> **URL** URL stands for Uniform Resource Locator, which is the standard address used to find a page or Web server, or other device on the Web or on the Internet. A URL is given to the device regardless of whether it is on a computer in the next state or two continents away

> **This Page Looks Different!** Don't panic if the home page you see for Paramount Pictures looks different than the one shown here. This difference illustrates an important lesson about Web pages—they change constantly. Because Paramount Pictures uses its home page to promote its movies and television shows, this page is subject to frequent change.

66 Lesson 11

4. Scroll down the page until you see the section titled **Paramount Television Presents**. Just below this title should be the link **Star Trek: Voyager**. Place the cursor on this link and click to jump to the Star Trek: Voyager Web page (see Figure 11.4).

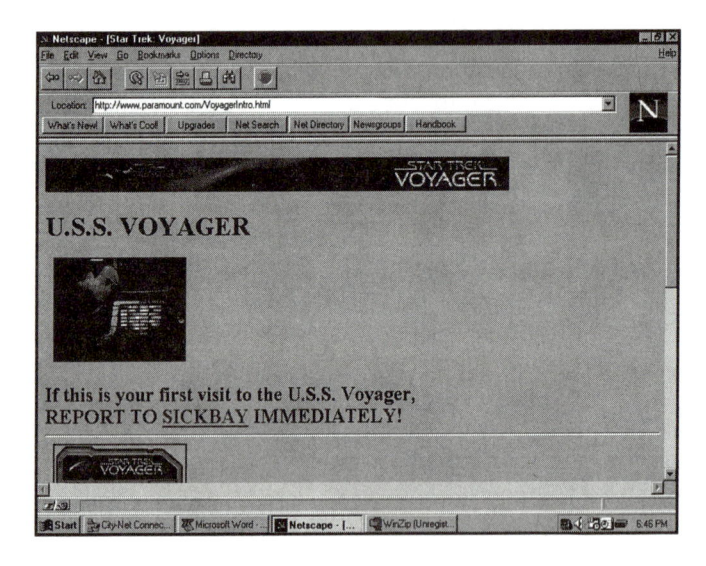

Figure 11.4   Star Trek: Voyager Web page.

> **Link**   A link connects text or pictures from one Web page to another Web page. Text links—made up of letters and words—are usually shown as a different color than ordinary text, and/or underlined in a Web page. Links are made up of hypertext. **Hypertext** is a system of extending textual information by embedding links in the text, which provide additional information about certain key words or phrases.

Spend some time looking over this Web page and its links. You might also try playing the audio clips that are included. This Web page is a good example of how text, pictures, and sound are used, and what you will see as you explore the Web further.

Netscape's History and Bookmarks Features

Netscape has two additional features you might find helpful — History and Bookmarks. After visiting a few Web pages, select Go, View History to see the History dialog box. Netscape's history feature is a temporary record of where you've been on the Internet. It's temporary because when you exit Netscape, the History dialog box is cleared.

To keep a permanent record of where you've been, select Bookmark, Add Bookmark. Bookmarks are a permanent record of sites and pages you've visited on the Internet. Your bookmarks will be there the next time you start Netscape.

If you want to get more detailed information on Netscape's History and Bookmark features, and about Netscape in general, take a look at another Que publication, the *10 Minute Guide to Netscape*.

In this lesson, you learned about the World Wide Web and how to use one of the most popular Web browsers, Netscape. In the next lesson, you learn about the Web browser designed specifically for Windows 95, the Internet Explorer.

Lesson 12: Using Microsoft Internet Explorer

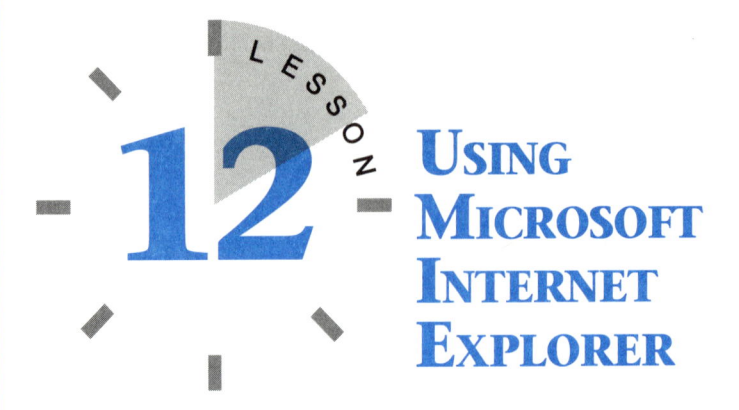

In this lesson, you learn how to use the Microsoft Internet Explorer Web browser.

Microsoft's Internet Explorer

Microsoft released Windows 95 with Internet support and several Internet utilities, some of which you've already learned about. In the previous lesson, you learned about the Web's most popular Web browser, Netscape. In this lesson, you learn about Microsoft's new Web browser, Internet Explorer. Compare the two Web browsers to see which one you prefer.

Before you can use Internet Explorer, you need to get a copy and install it. If you purchased the Windows 95 add-on product, Microsoft Plus!, you already have a copy of Internet Explorer. If you used the Microsoft Plus! Internet Setup Wizard (also called the Internet Jumpstart Kit) to set up your connection to your service provider, you have already installed Internet Explorer. Skip ahead to the section in this lesson titled "Using Internet Explorer."

To get your copy of Internet Explorer:

1. Start Netscape, as you did in the previous lesson. Now open the File menu and choose Open Location. Enter:

    http://www.microsoft.com

These steps take you to the Microsoft Windows 95 home page (see Figure 12.1).

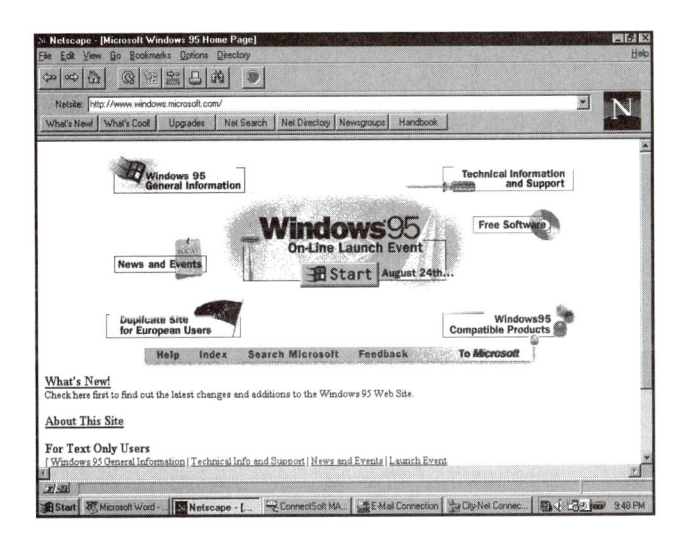

FIGURE 12.1 Microsoft Windows 95 home page.

2. Click the link Windows 95, click the link Free Software, and then click the link Internet Explorer. This sequence takes you to the Microsoft Internet Explorer Web page, as shown in Figure 12.2.

3. Follow the instructions on the page to download the file MSIE10.EXE, which is a self-decompressing archive file.

4. When the download is completed, copy MSIE10.EXE to its own directory, and then run it just as you do any other EXE file. When the file decompresses, MSIE10.EXE automatically begins installing Internet Explorer. Follow the prompts to complete the installation.

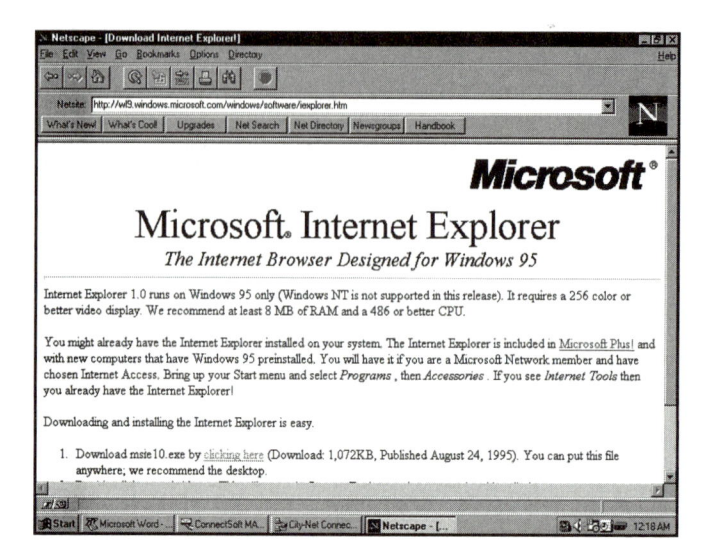

FIGURE 12.2 Microsoft Internet Explorer Web page.

USING INTERNET EXPLORER

When you installed the Internet Explorer (either through Microsoft Plus! or using MSIE10.EXE), a new icon was placed on your desktop during the installation, labeled **The Internet** (see Figure 12.3).

You use this icon to start Internet Explorer.

1. Double-click the The Internet icon to start Internet Explorer. If you're not already logged in with your provider, you are prompted to log in by the Dial-Up Networking Connection to your provider.

2. When Internet Explorer starts, it automatically loads the home page of the Microsoft Network as its home page (see Figure 12.4). Take time to explore the Microsoft Web site by jumping to some of the other links on this page—such as the New User Tutorial (the **New to the**

Internet, Click Here link) or Internet Searches and Links (the **Explore the Internet—Searches, Links, and Tools** link).

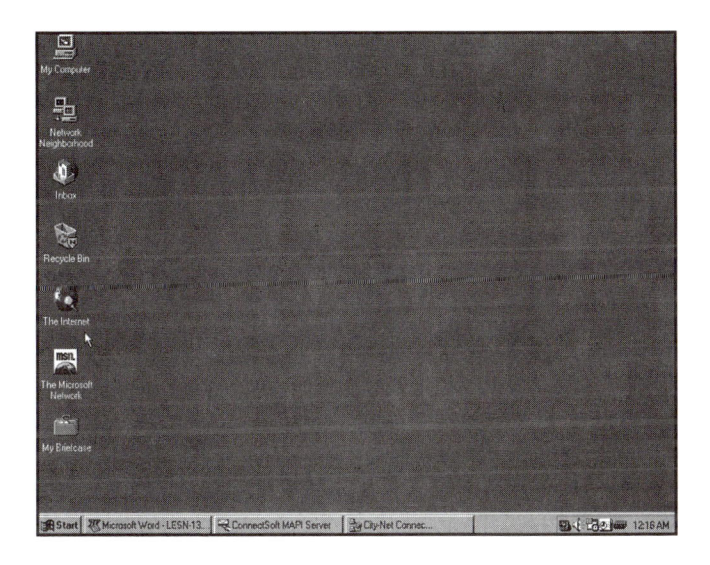

FIGURE 12.3   The Internet desktop icon.

3. To jump to a new Web site, open the File menu and choose Open. Enter the following URL in the Open Internet Address dialog box:

   http://www.hbohomevideo.com

   This URL takes you to HBO's home page on the Web, where you can view and listen to several interesting pages.

> **HBO Didn't Appear!** Most URLs are case sensitive; make sure you typed HBO's URL exactly as it is shown above, *not*:
>
> **http://www.HBOhomeVideo.com**
>
> Also note that the characters following http: are forward slashes (//), not backslashes (\\). Make sure you did *not* type:
>
> **http:\\www.hbohomevideo.com**
>
> If you verify the URL and you're still having trouble, maybe the Web site has its maximum number of visitors right now. Web sites *do* have limits (different for each site), and busy sites reach their limit often. All you can do is try again later.

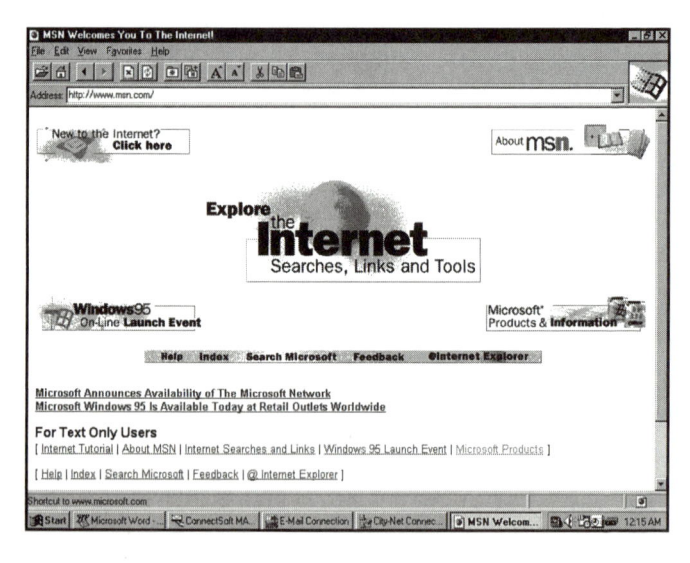

FIGURE 12.4   The Microsoft Network home page.

Internet Explorer's Toolbar

Notice the toolbar across the top of Internet Explorer's screen. It's made up of 13 icons that are preprogrammed with some of the most commonly used commands. Table 12.1 explains each icon's purpose.

TABLE 12.1 INTERNET EXPLORER TOOLBAR ICONS

Icon	Name	Description
	Open	Opens the Open Internet Address dialog box, where you can enter a URL.
	Open Start Page	Reloads the Internet Explorer's home page.
	Back	Takes you to the preceding page.
	Forward	Takes you to the next page.
	Stop	Stops a graphic from loading to the currently viewed page.
	Refresh	Restarts the loading of graphic images to the currently viewed page.
	Open Favorites	Opens the folder (window) containing your Favorite Page shortcuts.
	Add To Favorites	Allows you to add the URL of the current page to your list of Favorite Pages.
	Use Larger Font	Makes the text you are viewing larger.
	Use Smaller Font	Makes the text you are viewing smaller.

Lesson 12

Icon	Name	Description
✂	Cut	Cuts text (standard Windows editing command).
📋	Copy	Copies text (standard Windows editing command).
📋	Paste	Pastes cut or copied text (standard Windows editing command).

Some of these icons you probably already know how to use, such as the three editing icons: Cut, Copy, and Paste. Here's how to use the remaining icons, starting from left to right:

1. Click the Open icon to open the Open Internet Address window (see Figure 12.5).

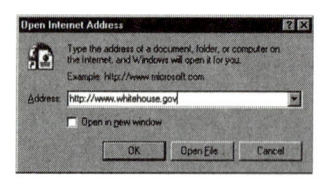

Figure 12.5 Open Internet Address window.

2. Enter the URL for the desired Internet address. Choose OK.

> **TIP** **Entering a URL** Another way to enter a URL is simply to type it in the address bar, which is located below the toolbar. To clear the address bar, click the URL that is currently displayed, and press the Backspace key. Type in the URL of the page you want to jump to and then press the Enter key. (You can simply highlight and type over the current URL, and then press Enter.)

3. Click the Open Start Page icon and you redisplay Internet Explorer's home page.

When you want to review previous pages you've viewed, use the Forward and Back icons. Think of it this way: If you've viewed five Web pages and you're on the fifth page, click Back and you return to the fourth page. Click Back again and you go back to the third page. Now click Forward and you return to the fourth page.

You can use the Stop and Refresh icons in tandem. When you jump to a Web page, the text and graphic images on that page are downloaded to your PC's Web browser. As Internet Explorer gets the text and graphic images, it starts to display them. If there are numerous graphic images or if the files are large, Internet Explorer may take a few seconds or a few minutes to receive all of the image files. Click the Stop icon to stop the download of graphic images. Internet Explorer displays the page's text and any complete images it has received. If you want to restart the download of the page to see it in its entirety, click the Refresh icon and the page is downloaded again.

Lesson 13 describes the Open Favorites and Add To Favorites icons in detail. You use the Open Favorites icon to display the folder containing the Favorite Page shortcuts that you've created (see Figure 12.6). We created all four shortcut icons shown in Figure 12.6.

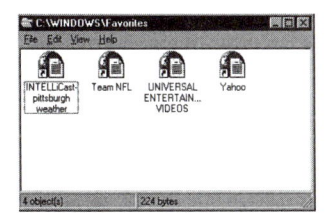

FIGURE 12.6 Folder containing Favorite Page shortcuts.

The Add To Favorites icon opens the Add To Favorites window, which you use to create Favorite Page shortcuts (see Figure 12.7). Adding Favorite Page icons is described in detail in Lesson 13.

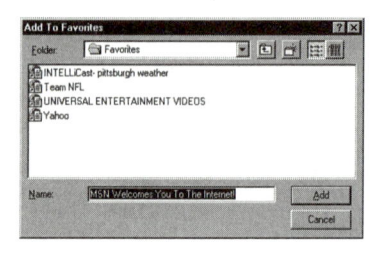

Figure 12.7 Add To Favorites window.

You can use the next two icons, Use Larger Font and Use Smaller Font, to increase or decrease the size of on-screen text. You can adjust the text fonts to five different sizes; use these icons to adjust the on-screen text to the size you are most comfortable with.

The last three icons, Cut, Copy, and Paste, are the standard Windows icons for performing these text-editing functions.

Changing the Appearance of Internet Explorer

Internet Explorer enables you to make a few changes to its appearance to allow you to view more of its display screen. You can remove its toolbar, address bar, and status bar using the View menu.

Open the View menu, and place or remove a check mark in front of **Toolbar**, **Address Bar**, and **Status Bar** to display or remove each option. Figures 12.8 and 12.9 show "before" and "after" views of the Internet Explorer screen.

USING MICROSOFT INTERNET EXPLORER 77

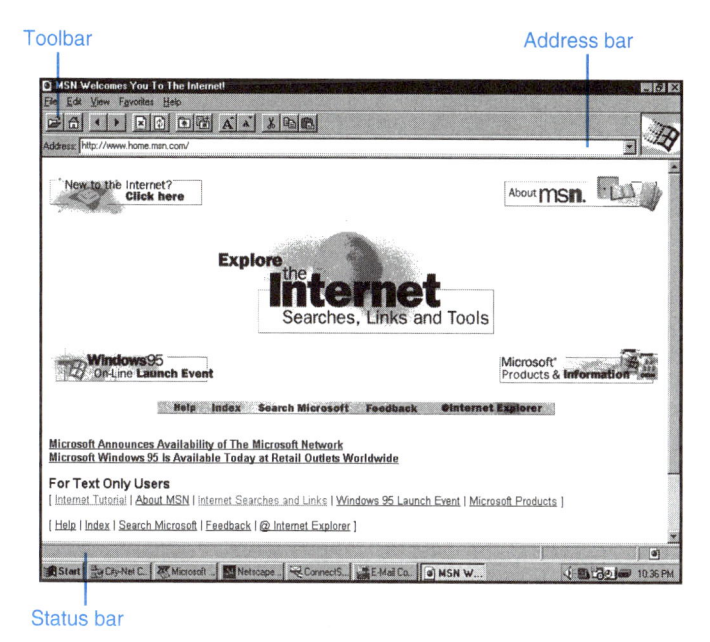

FIGURE 12.8 Internet Explorer with toolbar, address bar, and status bar.

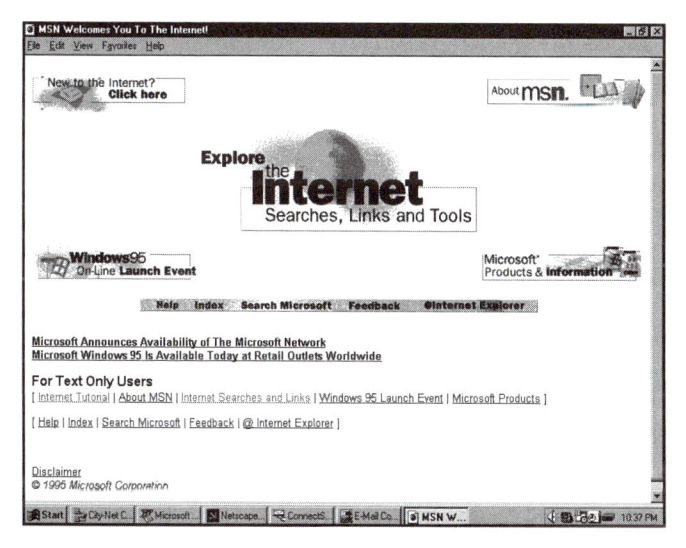

FIGURE 12.9 Internet Explorer without toolbar, address bar, and status bar.

In this lesson, you learned about Microsoft's Internet Explorer Web browser, how to get it, install it, and briefly how to use it. In the next lesson, you learn how to place markers on certain Web pages you visit so that you can easily return to them.

LESSON 13
SETTING BOOKMARKS AND MARKING FAVORITE PAGES

In this lesson, you learn how to keep track of Web pages you visit using Netscape's Bookmark feature and Internet Explorer's Favorite Pages feature.

USING NETSCAPE'S BOOKMARKS

Over the next few months, if you spend a fair amount of time "surfin' the Net," you will likely visit hundreds of Web sites. Keeping track of the ones you want to revisit could be a problem if not for the Bookmark feature built in to Netscape.

> **Bookmark** A bookmark is a placeholder, whether it is something you place between the pages of a book, or something you use to track pages you have visited on the Web. With Netscape, you can keep a list of these bookmarks—URLs you would like to return to.

To place a bookmark in Netscape:

1. Open the File menu and choose Open Location. In the Open Location dialog box, enter:

    http://www.planetreebok.com

LESSON 13

If you haven't guessed by now, this is Reebok's home page (see Figure 13.1).

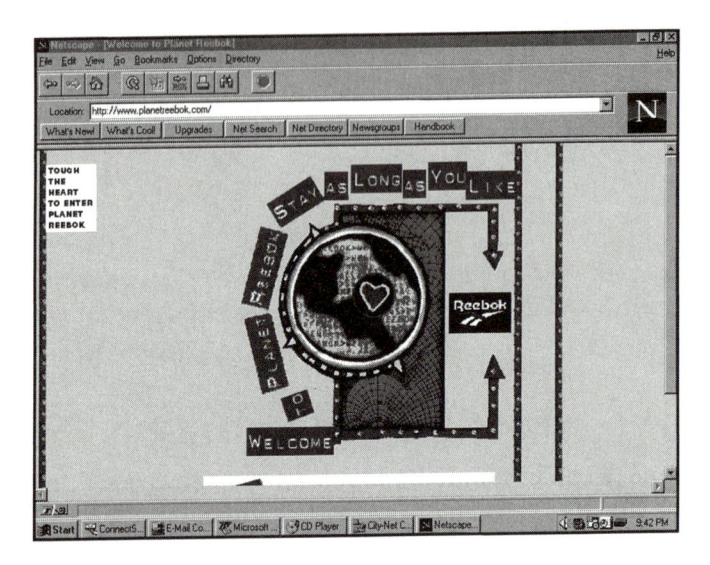

FIGURE 13.1 Reebok's home page.

2. Open the Bookmarks menu and choose Add Bookmark to place this URL in your bookmark list.

EDITING BOOKMARKS

Netscape also allows you to edit the items in your bookmark list.

1. Open the File menu and choose Open Location. In the Open Location dialog box, enter:

   http://espnet.sportszone.com

   This is ESPN's home page. If you're any kind of sports nut, this is the place to start on the Web (see Figure 13.2).

Setting Bookmarks and Marking Favorite Pages 81

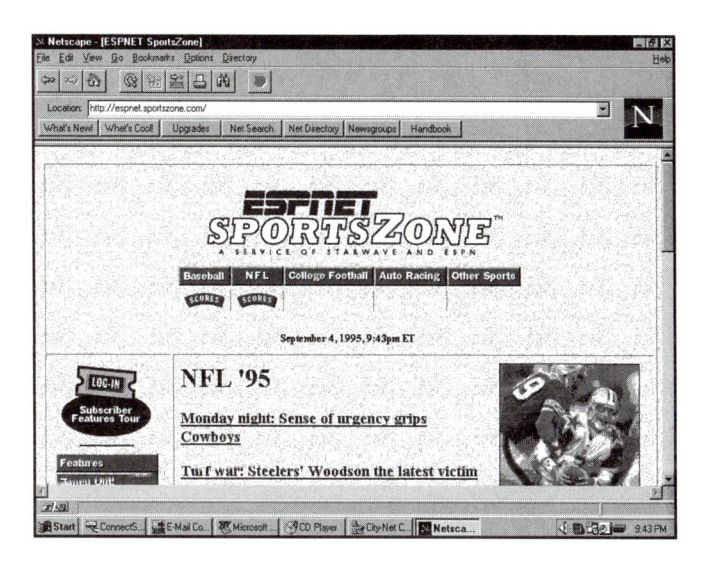

Figure 13.2 ESPNET SportsZone home page.

2. Open the Bookmarks menu and choose Add Bookmark to place this URL in your bookmark list.

3. Open the Bookmarks menu and choose View Bookmarks to open the Netscape Bookmarks window (see Figure 13.3).

4. Select ESPNET SportsZone. Open the Item menu and choose Properties to open the Bookmark Properties sheet (see Figure 13.4).

5. The title **ESPNET Sportszone** should be highlighted (if it's not, highlight it). Delete this title and enter **ESPN Home Page**. Choose OK and your bookmark listing changes.

Most of the Web pages you include in your bookmark lists will likely not need to be edited. But ocassionally, you will encounter Web pages where the author has created an obscure title, a very long title, or has actually neglected to give it a title. When no title is given, the URL becomes the title. By editing the title of your bookmark, you can give it a more meaningful title.

FIGURE 13.3 The Netscape Bookmarks window.

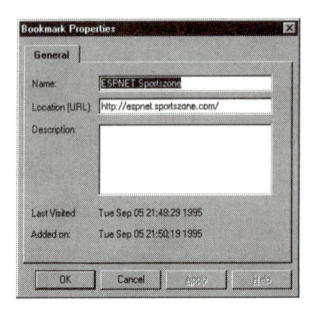

FIGURE 13.4 Bookmark Properties sheet.

CREATING BOOKMARK MENUS

Creating and editing bookmarks is not all Netscape lets you do. You can also create menu titles, or what Netscape calls **headers**. To create a header along with the two bookmarks you added earlier:

1. Open the Bookmarks menu and choose View Bookmarks to open the Netscape Bookmarks window.

Setting Bookmarks and Marking Favorite Pages 83

2. Select ESPN Home Page. Open the Item menu and choose Insert Header to open the Bookmark Properties sheet. In the **Name** field, delete New Header and enter Sports. Choose OK. The new header **Sports** appears below **ESPN Home Page**.

3. Click ESPN Home Page, hold down the left mouse button, drag it down to the header **Sports**, and release the mouse button. This action places the **ESPN Home Page** bookmark under the header **Sports** (see Figure 13.5).

Figure 13.5 ESPN Home Page under the Sports header.

4. Close the Netscape Bookmarks window. Select the Home icon to return to Netscape's home page. From the Netscape menu bar, choose Bookmarks. Notice that the bookmarks have changed. Choose Sports and you'll see the header submenu appear displaying the **ESPN Home Page** bookmark (see Figure 13.6). Choose the ESPN Home Page bookmark to jump to ESPN's home page.

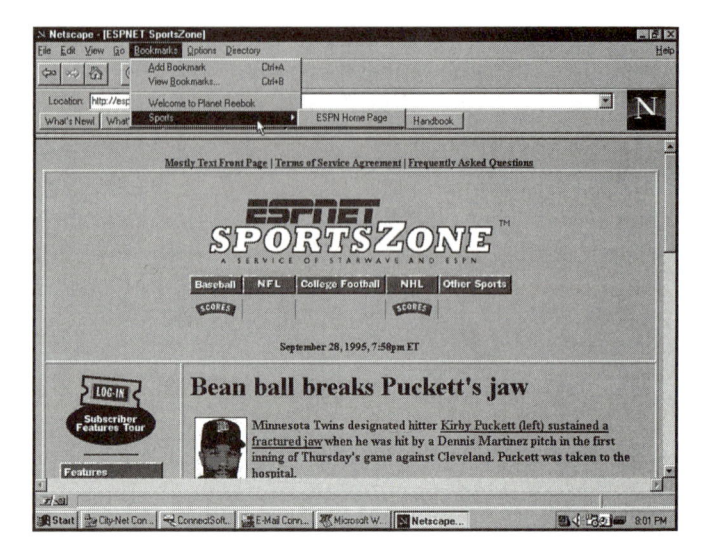

FIGURE 13.6 Sports header submenu.

Recording Your Favorite Pages in Internet Explorer

Microsoft's Internet Explorer also gives you a means of recording Web sites you've visited. In Internet Explorer, bookmarks are called **Favorite Pages**, instead of bookmarks. After starting Internet Explorer, to create a Favorite Page:

1. Open the File menu and choose Open. The Open Internet Address dialog box appears. Enter the following URL:

    http://www.nflhome.com

    Choose OK. In a few seconds, you should be at the home page of the National Football League.

Setting Bookmarks and Marking Favorite Pages 85

> **TIP**
>
> **Enter the URL Directly** Just as you could type the URL in Netscape's Location field without having to open the Open Location dialog box, you can also type URLs directly into Internet Explorer's address box to save time.

2. Open the Favorites menu and choose Add to Favorites to open the Add to Favorites window (see Figure 13.7). Select the Add button to create this Favorite Page.

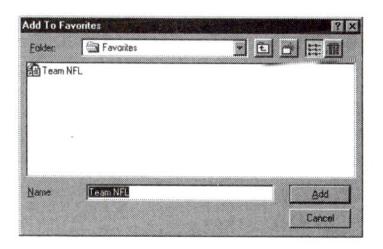

Figure 13.7 Adding a Favorite Page entry.

3. Choose Favorites again from the Internet Explorer menu bar and you'll see that a shortcut has been created for this Web page (see Figure 13.8).

If you haven't guessed by now, Favorite Pages are really Windows 95 shortcuts, created inside a special folder called Favorites, which is created in your Windows folder. Because they are shortcuts in a folder, you can manipulate them the same way you would any other group of shortcuts in a folder. You can open the Favorites menu and choose Open Favorites and change the appearance of your Internet Explorer shortcuts using the View menu option the same way you might change any folder full of icons (e.g., change large icons to a text listing). You can also drag them to your desktop the same as you would any other shortcut icon.

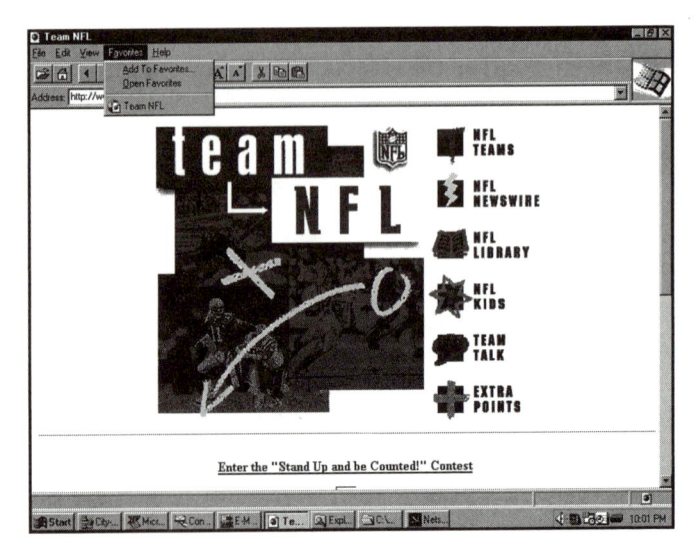

FIGURE 13.8 Favorites folder containing shortcuts.

> **TIP**
> **Drag Shortcuts to Desktop** If there are favorite places you regularly visit, you might find it helpful to drag the shortcuts to your desktop where they are more accessible.

> **If You're Using Both Netscape and Internet Explorer** One problem arises with dragging shortcuts to your desktop if you have both Netscape and Internet Explorer installed on your PC. Shortcuts in Internet Explorer are actually files with the extension HTM. When you install Netscape, it creates a file association between Netscape and files with the extension HTM so that if you double-click a file with the HTM extension, it starts Netscape. So if you have both browsers installed, your desktop shortcuts will, in fact, start Netscape and not Internet Explorer.

Setting Bookmarks and Marking Favorite Pages   87

In this lesson, you learned how to record Web pages you've visited by creating bookmarks in Netscape and Favorite Pages in Internet Explorer. In the next lesson, you learn how to locate Web pages using various search programs.

LESSON 14

SEARCHING THE INTERNET USING SEARCH ENGINES

In this lesson, you learn how to search for Web pages using two of the Internet's best search engines—Yahoo and Lycos.

WHAT IS A SEARCH ENGINE?

So far, all of the Web pages you've seen in this book have been pages you've been directed to in various lessons. But you don't have to wait around for someone to tell you about Web pages and where to find them. You can locate them yourself by using a search engine. A **search engine** (on the World Wide Web) is a program that analyzes Web page titles and keeps track of the information they contain. It allows you to enter a search request, called a **query**, and then gives you a list of Web pages that matches your query. Two of the most popular search engines on the Web are Yahoo and Lycos.

YAHOO

Yahoo, which was started a few years ago at Stanford by two graduate students, now ranks as one of the most popular Web search engines. Both Netscape and Internet Explorer contain built-in links to Yahoo so you can get there quickly.

To get to Yahoo in Netscape:

1. Select the **Net Directory**. This takes you to Netscape's Internet Directory page.

Searching the Internet Using Search Engines 89

> **I Don't Have Any Directory Buttons!** If Netscape's directory buttons don't appear across your screen, you may have turned them off. Select the Options menu and make sure there is a checkmark in front of the menu item **Directory Buttons**. If you don't want to turn directory buttons on, the URL for Yahoo is **http://www.yahoo.com**. You might want to place it in your bookmark list.

2. You'll see that the first link is to Yahoo (see Figure 14.1). Click the Yahoo link to go to Yahoo.

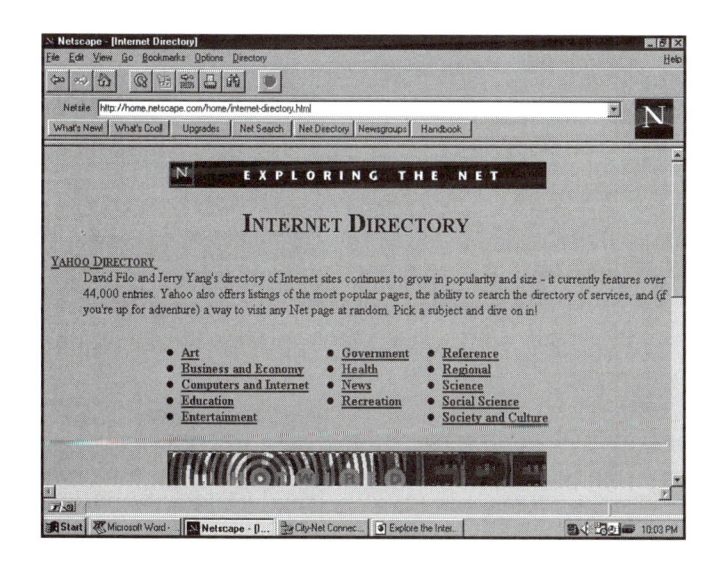

Figure 14.1 Netscape's Internet Directory page.

To get to Yahoo using Internet Explorer:

1. At Internet Explorer's home page, they call it their Start Page, click the link in the center of the screen, Explore the Internet—Searches, Links, and Tools. This link takes you to the Internet Explorer's Explore the Internet page shown in Figure 14.2.

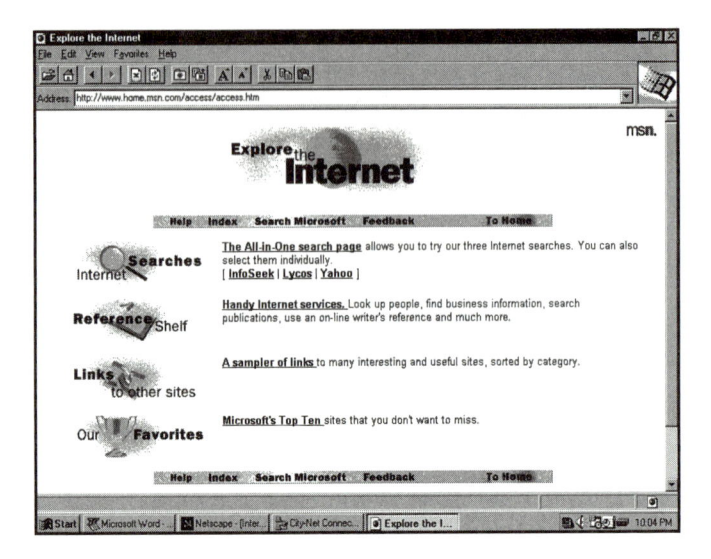

FIGURE 14.2 Internet Explorer's Explore the Internet page.

2. In the area near the top of the page labeled, **Internet Searches**, you'll see a link to **Yahoo** (along with links to two other search engines, one of which, **Lycos**, is covered later in this lesson). Click Yahoo to jump to the Yahoo home page.

Of the two browser links, Netscape's takes you directly to Yahoo. Internet Explorer's presents its own query page and passes that query to Yahoo. Internet Explorer's arrangement prevents you from using Yahoo's query options, but you can get around this by entering the URL for Yahoo and going directly to Yahoo's home page.

http://www.yahoo.com

By jumping directly to Yahoo's home page you now have access to Yahoo's own query screen, complete with the options you see in Figure 14.3.

Searching the Internet Using Search Engines 91

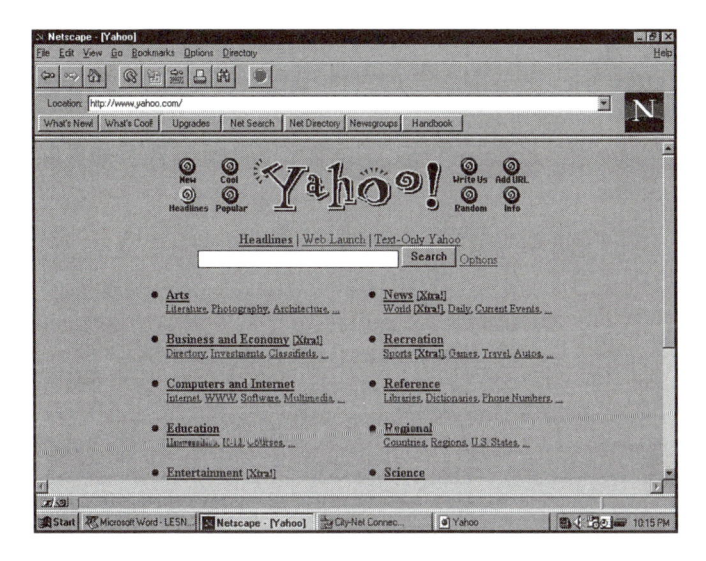

Figure 14.3 Yahoo search engine home page.

Yahoo works in two ways: It keeps a categorized list of Web pages organized under 14 major categories and it allows you to enter a search query. The Yahoo categories are:

- Arts
- Computers and Internet
- Entertainment
- Health
- Recreation
- Regional
- Social Science

- Business and Economy
- Education
- Government
- News
- Reference
- Science
- Society and Culture

Searching by Category

Because Yahoo already has a long list of Web pages organized by category, searching Yahoo by category is done by stepping through links along the established categories and subcategories.

92　LESSON 14

For example, suppose you want to locate Web pages that contain information on the Grand Canyon. Here's how you would use Yahoo:

1. At the Yahoo home page, click the Regional link. Clicking this link takes you to Yahoo's Regional page.
2. At the Regional page, click the U.S. States link to go to the Regional:U.S. States page.
3. At the Regional:U.S. States page, click the Arizona link to go to the Regional:U.S. States:Arizona page.
4. At the Regional:U.S. States:Arizona page, click the Grand Canyon link to go to the Regional:U.S. States:Arizona: Grand Canyon page, which is the object of your search (see Figure 14.4).

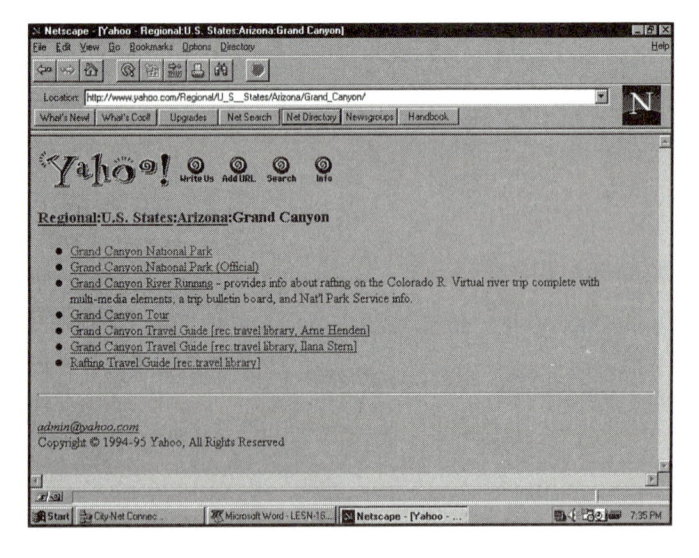

FIGURE 14.4 Regional:U.S. States:Arizona:Grand Canyon page.

At this point, you're free to examine any or all of the Grand Canyon links. If you have a few minutes, click the Grand Canyon Tour link. Besides receiving a wealth of interesting facts about the world's most popular canyon, you'll also see breathtaking photos, like the one shown in Figure 14.5 (The URL for this is **http://turnpike.net/metro/H/hud/MESA7.JPG**.)

FIGURE 14.5 View of the Grand Canyon

FINDING A TOPIC BY KEYWORD

Yahoo also allows you to conduct a search by keyword:

1. At the Yahoo home page, enter a keyword in the query field and select the Search button. For this example, enter the keyword **eclipse**, as in solar eclipse.

2. The results of your query will appear in a few seconds (see Figure 14.6). You can scroll down the page until you find a section for **Science:Astronomy**, or you can examine what Yahoo found when searching for the keyword "eclipse."

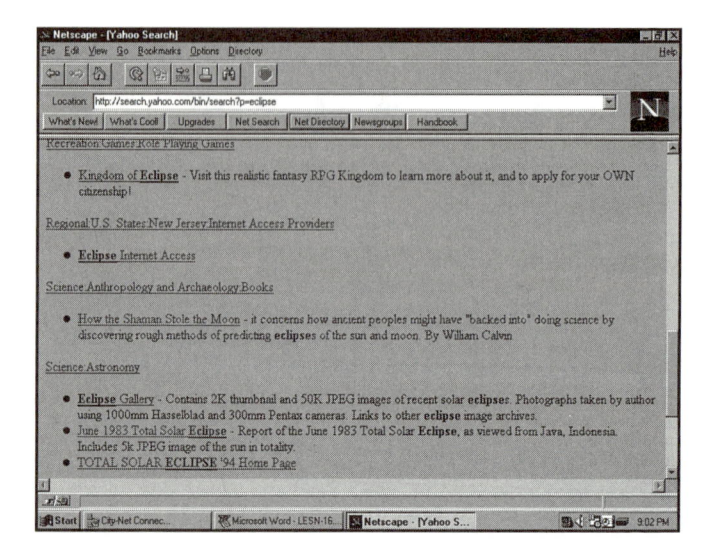

FIGURE 14.6 Results of the Yahoo query on eclipse.

Yahoo also allows you to modify your search parameters (see Figure 14.7).

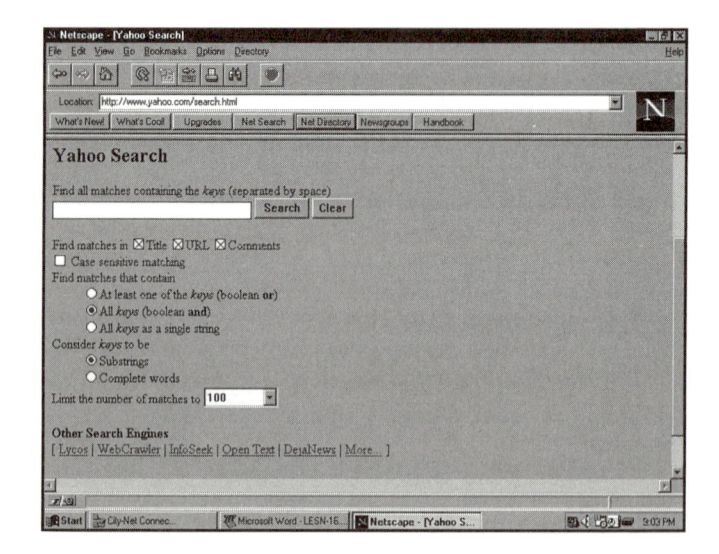

FIGURE 14.7 Yahoo's option settings.

The options are most often used when:

- You want to search on multiple keywords and are concerned about the query searching for either word (e.g., *keyword1* **or** *keyword2*) or the query searching for both words (e.g., *keyword1* **and** *keyword2*). An example here would be if you searched on the keywords "star trek". By default, Yahoo would search for instances of "star" or instances of "trek" and would consider a match on anything that has either word. But if you did your search on "star and trek" it would only consider a match pages that contained the words (together) "star" "trek".

- You want the keyword treated as a partial word (substring) or a complete word.

- You want to increase the number of results returned in the event they exceed the default of 100.

LYCOS

Another popular Internet search engine is **Lycos**, which is run by Carnegie Mellon University in Pittsburgh.

You can find Lycos at:

http://www.lycos.com/

Lycos is a very large database and works like the keyword search engine in Yahoo (see Figure 14.8). It has most of the same options as Yahoo for modifying your query parameters. Select the Options link to see the options page as shown in Figure 14.9.

If you're wondering which search engine to use, here are a couple guidelines: If you're searching on a topic that you think is mainstream, try Yahoo first. It's smaller and a lot faster than Lycos. If, on the other hand, your search parameters appear somewhat obscure, or the topic is not necessarily something that pops up in everyday conversation, then Lycos will generally produce better results because its database is more than 10 times larger than Yahoo's. But bear in mind, Lycos can be a lot slower than Yahoo, too.

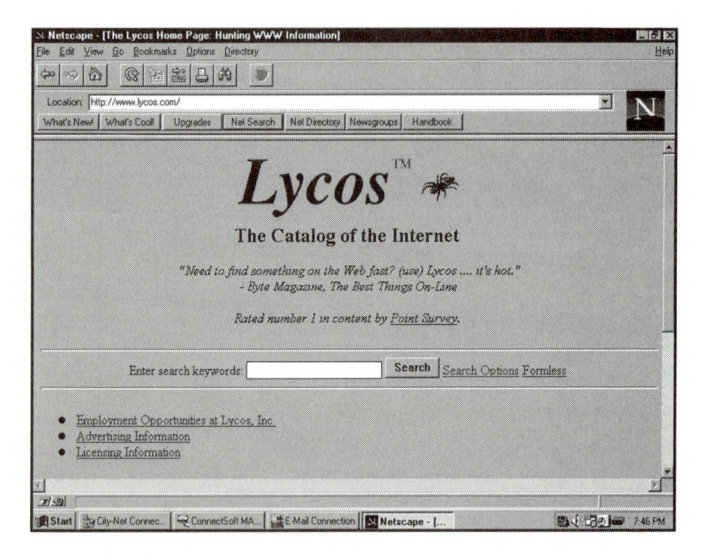

FIGURE 14.8 Lycos home page.

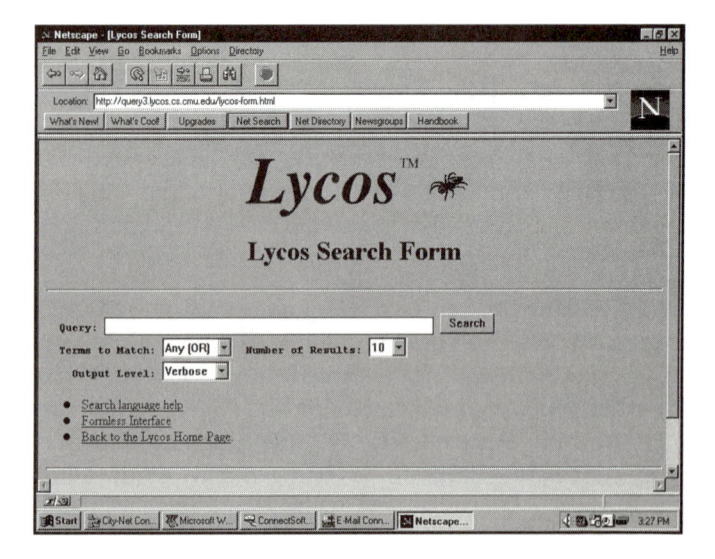

FIGURE 14.9 Lycos search options.

If Yahoo and Lycos don't meet your needs, here are a few other search engines you can try:

Search Engine	Address
WebCrawler	**http://www.webcrawler.com**
Infoseek	**http://www2.infoseek.com**
Open Text	**http://www.opentext.com:8080/omw.html**
New Riders' Official WWW Yellow Pages	**http://www.mcp.com/nrp/wwwyp**
Galaxy	**http://www.einet.net/search.html**

WebCrawler—WebCrawler is the only other "robot" search engine in this group besides Lycos. Like Lycos, it uses a search technique that actually visits other Internet sites to gather information about its database. This technique produces a fairly large, fairly comprehensive database of Internet sites, pages, and information.

Infoseek—Infoseek is a commercial search engine that boasts a very large following, or at least a very busy search engine (1 million search requests per day). It's geared more towards commercial users (large commercial database; quick turnaround).

Open Text—Open Text has allied itself with Yahoo to combine their services. It too is aimed more at mainstream, popular topics in its search database.

New Riders' Official WWW Yellow Pages—This is the online version of the NRP WWW Yellow Pages. It is, by design, a tool used only to search the World Wide Web, and has a very extensive and diverse Web database.

Galaxy—Galaxy has one of the most interesting home pages that tries to supply something for everyone. It's fairly popular because of its home page and continues to be a popular search engine for popular subjects.

In this lesson, you learned how to use two of the most popular search engines used on the World Wide Web, Yahoo and Lycos. In the next lesson, you learn about viewing certain types of graphic files used in Web pages.

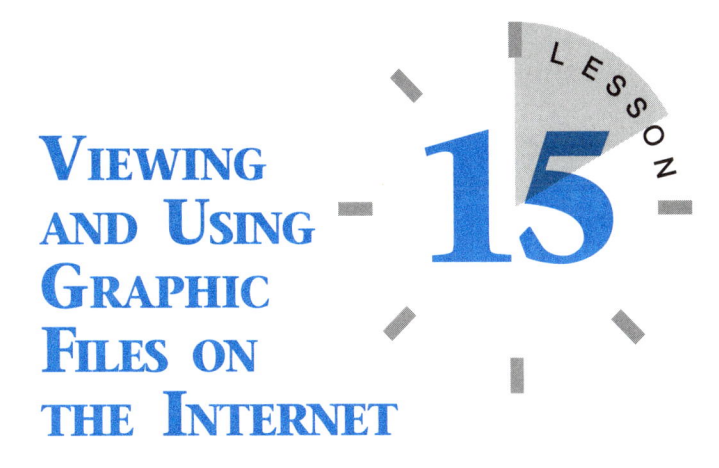

LESSON 15
VIEWING AND USING GRAPHIC FILES ON THE INTERNET

In this lesson, you learn about the types of graphic files you are likely to encounter on the Internet.

VIEWING GRAPHIC FILES

Both of the Web browsers you've looked at in previous lessons, Internet Explorer and Netscape, have no trouble displaying the majority of the types of graphic files you are likely to encounter on most Web pages—usually GIF and JPEG (also listed as JPG) files.

Using either browser, go to the following Web site to see how GIF and JPEG are displayed (see Figure 15.1):

http://www.netaxs.com/people/tporett/

Netscape gives you the ability to save any graphic file you view on a Web page. Here's an example:

1. In Netscape, open the File menu and choose Open Location. Jump to the following Web page by entering the following URL in the Open Location dialog box:

    http://www.nflhome.com/teams/49ers/49ers.html

    This is the home page of the 1995 Super Bowl Champion San Francisco 49ers (see Figure 15.2).

100   LESSON 15

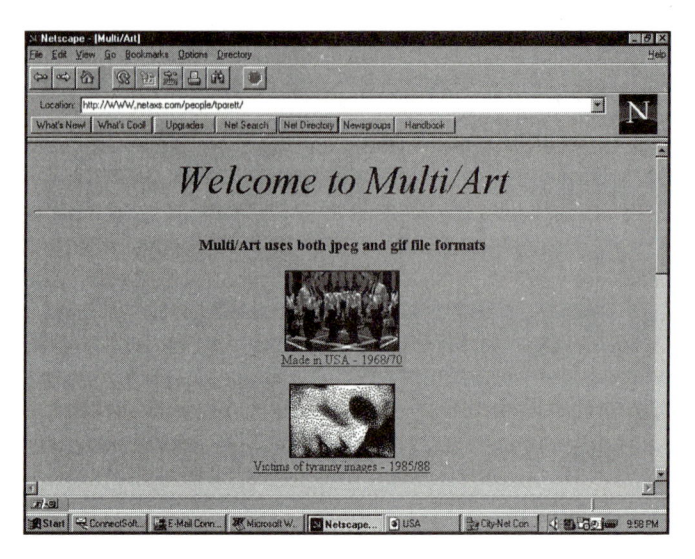

FIGURE 15.1   Web site containing GIF and JPEG files.

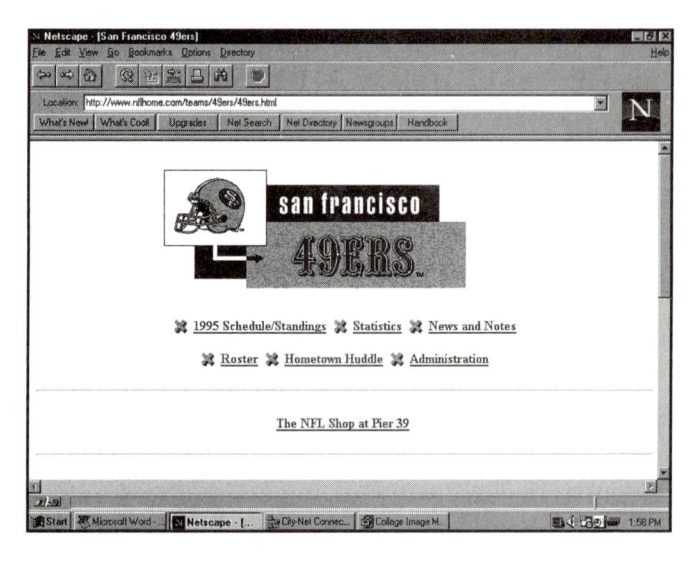

FIGURE 15.2   San Francisco 49ers home page.

2. To save the graphic image in the center of the screen (the one with the picture of the helmet and the words San Francisco 49ERS), right-click the image. The menu shown in Figure 15.3 appears.

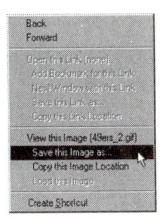

FIGURE 15.3 Netscape's Navigation and File menu.

3. Choose Save this Image as to bring up the Netscape Save As dialog box (see Figure 15.4).

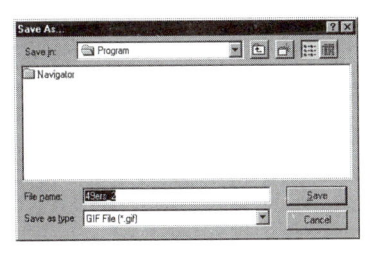

FIGURE 15.4 Netscape's Save As dialog box.

4. Select the Save button to save the file to your PC. If you do not specify a different drive or path, the file will be saved in your Netscape application folder.

Now you're probably saying, "So what, I saved the GIF file. Now what can I do with it?" Well, here's how to take that GIF file and turn it into wallpaper for your Windows desktop:

1. Select the Start button on the taskbar and choose Programs, Windows Explorer. Use the Windows Explorer to locate the GIF file you just saved using Netscape.

2. When you locate the file, double-click it. This causes Windows' file association properties to start the application associated with the file type GIF, which should be the Internet Explorer, and load the file 49ers_2.gif (see Figure 15.5).

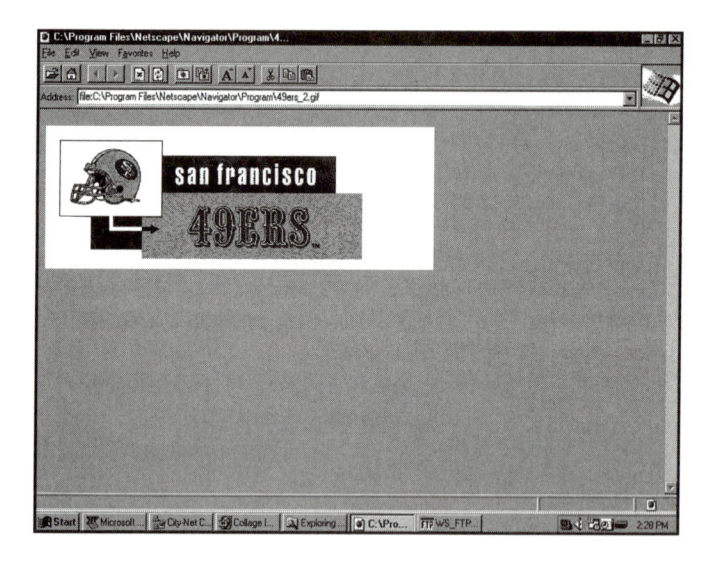

FIGURE 15.5 Internet Explorer with the file 49ers_2.gif.

> **I Don't Have Internet Explorer!** Don't panic. You can use most GIF viewers/converters to convert a GIF file into Windows wallpaper. Use your FTP utility to download the file gif2bmp.zip from the Gatekeeper FTP site. It's located in the /pub/msdos/micro/win3/desktop directory.

3. In the Internet Explorer application, open the File menu and choose Save As. From the **Save as type** drop-down list, select Bitmap (*.bmp).

4. From the **Save in** drop-down list, select your C:\ drive and select the Windows folder. This folder is where you want the BMP file saved. Now select the Save button.

5. Open the File menu and choose Exit to close Internet Explorer.

To tell Windows to use the newly saved BMP file as wallpaper:

1. Minimize or close any applications you have running so that your desktop is clear.

2. Right-click anywhere on your desktop to open the Desktop menu. Choose Properties to open the Display Properties sheet. If the Background page is not displayed, select the Background tab.

3. In the Wallpaper list, select 49ers_2. Make sure the Center Display radio button is selected. Choose OK to save your background wallpaper selection. The Display Properties sheet closes and your new wallpaper appears (see Figure 15.6).

FIGURE 15.6   San Francisco 49ers wallpaper.

LESSON 15

Keep in mind a few things about wallpaper files. Some files are physically larger than others, which means that some will cover the entire background and others will only cover a portion of it, as you've seen here. As you view other Web pages, always be on the lookout for other files to use as wallpaper. For example, you could just as easily have gone to:

ftp://ugcs.caltech.edu/pub/gifs/Pakistan/k2.gif

And created the wallpaper picture you see in Figure 15.7.

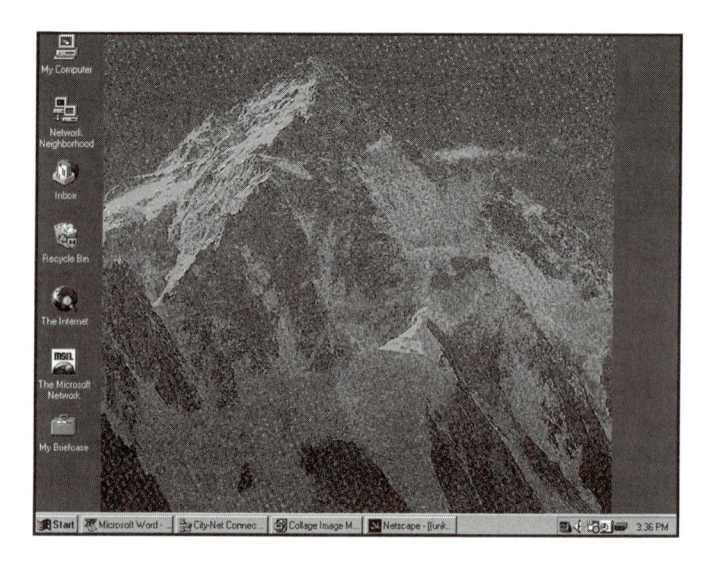

FIGURE 15.7 Mt. K2 as wallpaper.

In this lesson, you learned that you can do more with Web page graphic images than simply view them with your browser. In the next lesson, you learn about Web page audio.

Audio on the Internet—Audio and RealAudio™

Lesson 16

In this lesson, you learn about Internet audio and how to configure your browser to play RealAudio.

Audio on the Internet

Netscape and MS Internet Explorer can display the majority of the graphic files you're likely to encounter on the Web, plus play most of the audio files that are out there.

Follow these instructions to hear an example of a typical audio file:

1. In Netscape, open the File menu and choose Open Location. Jump to the following Web page by entering the following URL into the Open Location dialog box:

    http://www.paramount.com/ VoyagerIntro.html

    This page is the Star Trek Voyager home page created by Paramount Pictures (see Figure 16.1).

2. Scroll down the page until you see **A Message from Kate Mulgrew!**. There are links for two audio files, (au 8kHz 49k) and (11kHz 68k). Select one of these audio files to hear "A message from Kate Mulgrew."

LESSON 16

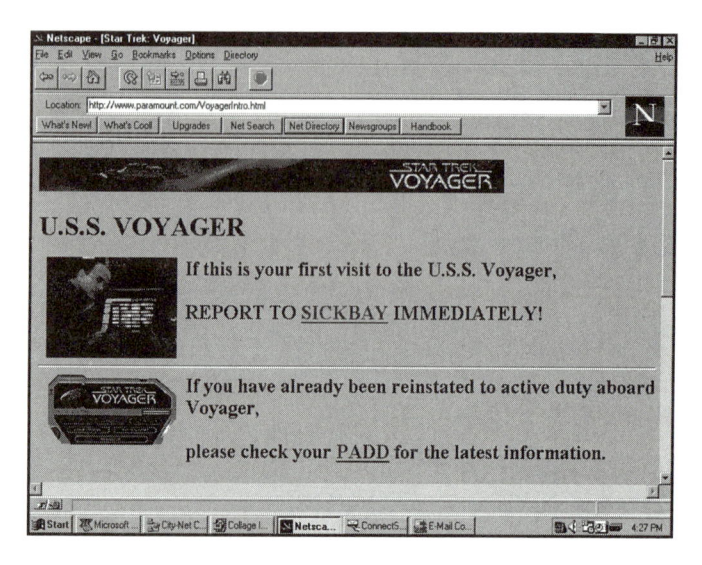

FIGURE 16.1 Star Trek Voyager home page.

> **I Don't Hear Anything!** In order to hear audio on your PC, you must have some mechanism to play audio files. The best audio comes from a sound card configured for Windows 95 and a pair of speakers. If you don't have a sound card, you may be able to use a PC speaker driver program to play audio files on the small speaker in your PC. However, these programs don't produce anywhere near the quality of sound that a sound card can produce. You can download a copy of the PC Speaker driver in Gatekeeper in /pub/micro/msdos/win3/sounds in the file SPEAK.EXE.

Before the file is played, it's downloaded to your computer. The larger of the two files takes slightly under 30 seconds to download with a 28.8 kbps connection. This problem has been one of the biggest problems facing Web audio; before you can play the file, you have to download it, and audio files that play more than just a few seconds of sound tend to be quite large. A 30-second audio clip can easily exceed 500K and take over three minutes to download over a 28.8 kbps connection.

Fortunately, a newer audio format, RealAudio, seems to have overcome the "download-before-playing" problem.

RealAudio™

RealAudio is one of the most amazing and interesting sound reproduction systems available on the Internet. It seems to solve one of the major problems in delivering multimedia sound over the Internet. With RealAudio, you can hear files that are 15 minutes long or longer in just a few seconds!

RealAudio compresses the audio stream as it's sent down the Internet to your computer and buffers the stream as it's received. This means that you hear the sound a few seconds after your computer receives it. Your computer always has a few seconds more of the stream than you have heard. While the sound this technology produces is a far cry from CD-quality, it produces sound that's good enough to use for news and information.

Rather than have an in-depth discussion of how this technology works, let's install RealAudio on your PC.

1. In Netscape, open the File menu and choose Open Location. Enter the following URL in the Open Location dialog box to jump to the following Web page:

    http://www.realaudio.com/

    This is the RealAudio home page (see Figure 16.2).

2. In the first paragraph, under the caption **RealAudio Player and Encoder**, click the Download link to go to the RealAudio Player Download Page (see Figure 16.3).

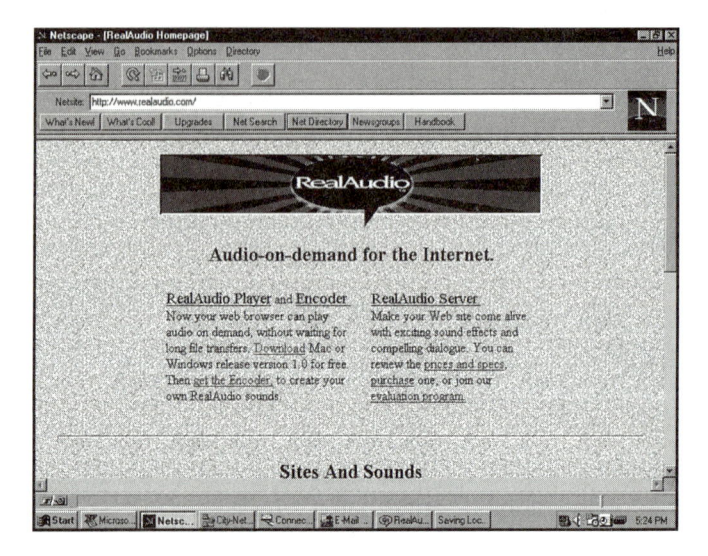

FIGURE 16.2 RealAudio home page.

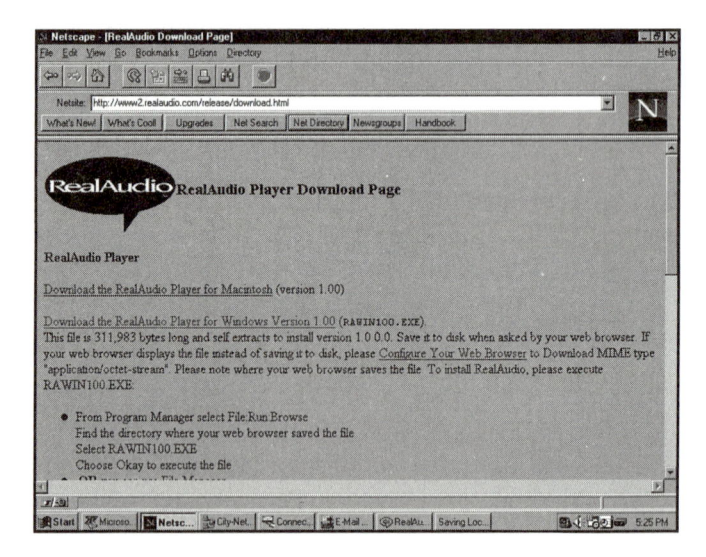

FIGURE 16.3 RealAudio Player Download Page.

3. Click the link Download the RealAudio Player for Windows Version 1.00 to download the file RAWIN100.EXE to your PC (see Figure 16.4).

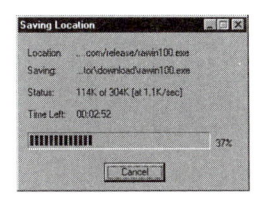

FIGURE 16.4   Downloading the RealAudio player.

> **Print the FAQs** It's helpful to print the RealAudio FAQ page and the RealAudio Player FAQ page. Both pages contain valuable information on configuring and troubleshooting RealAudio. To get to the RealAudio FAQ page, click the RealAudio Player FAQ link on the RealAudio Player Download Page. Click the Configure Your Web Browser link to get to the RealAudio Player FAQ page.

4. Open the Windows Explorer and locate the folder where Netscape saved the file you just downloaded (RAWIN100.EXE). If Netscape is still running, close it. Double-click RAWIN100.EXE and follow the prompts to automatically install RealAudio. Accept the default values during installation. RealAudio Player automatically configures itself as a Help App (see Lesson 18 for more information on Netscape Help Apps).

5. When the installation is completed, restart Netscape and go back to the RealAudio home page.

> **TIP — Create Bookmarks** You'll certainly save yourself a few headaches later if you create bookmarks as you go through each lesson. To return to Web pages you like, it's a lot easier to open the Bookmarks menu and choose Add Bookmark (or press Ctrl+A) than it is to go back through each lesson and try to locate each URL.

6. Scroll down to the **Sites and Sounds Section** to see some of the organizations currently using RealAudio. Click the ABC logo to jump to the ABC page. Select one of the available links, and then listen. In a few seconds, the RealAudio Player appears, as you see in Figure 16.5. A few seconds later, you should hear an audio report that lasts a few minutes.

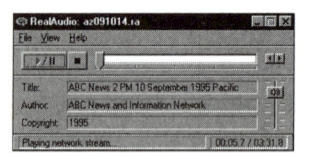

FIGURE 16.5 RealAudio Player playing audio report.

> **I Don't Hear Anything!** It's possible, for a variety of reasons too numerous to list here, that RealAudio doesn't work on your system. Go back and take a look at the two FAQ pages mentioned earlier to see if either page sheds any light on your audio problem. Also, double-check your installation procedure to make sure that you didn't skip any steps. Finally, open the Options menu and choose Preferences. From the **Set Preferences On** drop-down list, select Helper Applications. Check to make sure there is a reference to the RealAudio player and that Netscape is looking into the folder where the RealAudio player is installed. If everything checks out okay, you might want to check with your provider to make sure RealAudio is not being blocked by your provider.

If you started browsing the various sites and pages where RealAudio can be heard, you may have noticed that some pages require you to register for a free user account. RealAudio developers probably use this method to track the number of people on the Internet who use and listen to RealAudio. If you plan to use RealAudio in the future, go ahead and register.

If you haven't started browsing the RealAudio home page and its links, by all means do so. You'll be surprised by the long list of RealAudio sites on the **Sites** link. Be sure to visit the **Specials** site to hear the 39 minute broadcast of the 1937 Hindenburg disaster.

In this lesson, you learned about audio on the Web and the emerging technology, RealAudio. In the next lesson, you learn how to configure the Internet Explorer to work with a wider variety of file types.

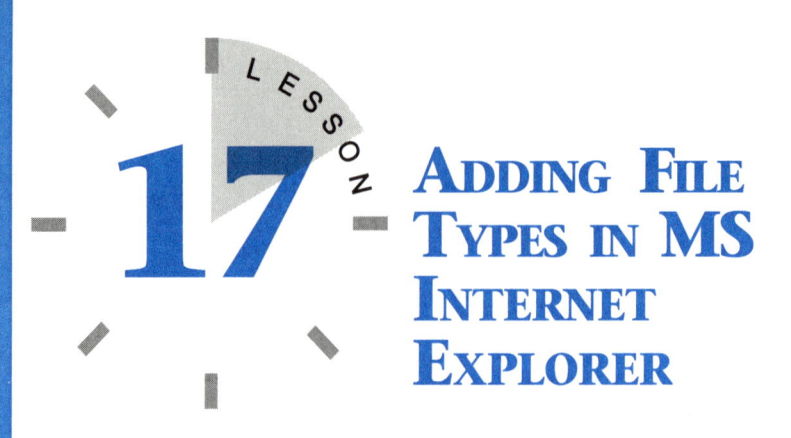

LESSON 17
Adding File Types in MS Internet Explorer

In this lesson, you learn how to configure MS Internet Explorer to display additional types of file formats.

Configuring File Types in Internet Explorer

MS Internet Explorer comes preconfigured to display most types of graphic files you will encounter while browsing the Web. However, as multimedia becomes a more popular tool used in creating Web pages, you will encounter graphic file types that Internet Explorer can't display without help. In the area of multimedia, full-motion video seems to be making a lot of headway onto the Web, and the prevalent file type seems to be MPEG (also called MPG).

> **MPEG** MPEG is a graphic format created by the Motion Picture Entertainment Group that specifies a format for creating and displaying full-motion video clips.

> **Multimedia** Multimedia is simply a mixture of several types of media, such as text, pictures (graphic files)—both still and motion pictures—and sound.

Adding File Types in MS Internet Explorer   113

You can configure Internet Explorer, like other Web browsers, to use other programs to help it play or display file formats that it can't play on its own.

Internet Explorer is very closely linked to the Windows 95 environment, so closely linked, in fact, that the changes that you make to allow it to work with other file formats are really made in the Windows 95 environment. In Windows 3.1, you use the Windows File Manager to "associate" a file type with a particular application (e.g., ZIP files are associated with WinZip or PKUNZIP). Once an association is made between a file type and an application, you can start that particular application by selecting (usually by double-clicking in a viewer type program like File Manager or Windows Explorer) a file of that file type. This association is exactly what you do now to associate the MPG file type with an application you will download from an FTP site. Once this association is made, this association will work in Internet Explorer and in the entire Windows 95 environment.

Obtaining an MPEG Viewer

Before you can configure either browser to display MPEG files, you need to obtain an MPEG viewer. You can download a MPEG viewer from the following Web page using either Netscape or Internet Explorer:

http://www.best.com/~johnp/resources.html

1. Jump to the Web page listed above. Click the VMPEG 1.7 link to download the designated viewer.

> **TIP** — **Download Files Quickly** Quite often, you'll see that specific files and programs have been placed in Web pages with links to FTP servers. These links were preset to allow you to download the files with your Web browser; you don't have to use an FTP program.

2. The file you're downloading, vmpeg.exe, is a self decompressing archive file (just like a ZIP file, except that you don't need PKUNZIP to decompress it). Copy vmpeg.exe into its own folder and run it the same as you would any other EXE file. The archived contents are decompressed.

3. To install VMPeg 1.7, select the Start button on the taskbar and choose Settings, Control Panel. In the Control Panel window, select the Add/Remove Programs icon to launch the Add/Remove Programs wizard. Follow the prompts and, during installation, accept the default values and prompts.

Associating the File Type MPEG/MPG

Before Internet Explorer can display MPEG files you locate on the Web, you must configure Internet Explorer to be able to use and display the MPEG (MPG) file type format:

1. Open the View menu and choose Options. In the Options dialog box, select the File Types tab.

2. Select the New Type button to open the Add New File Type dialog box.

3. In the **Description of Type** field, enter **MPEG Video**. Enter **.mpg** in the **Associated Extension** field. In the **Content Type (MIME)** drop-down list, select video/mpeg.

4. Select the New button to open the New Action dialog box. In the **Action** field, enter open. In the **Application used to perform action** field, enter **C:\Vmpeg\Vmpegwin.exe /play**. Adding the /play command will cause the video to begin playing after it downloads. If you don't want the video to start automatically, don't include the /play parameter. Choose OK to close the New Action dialog box. Select the **Always Show Extension** check box (see Figure 17.1).

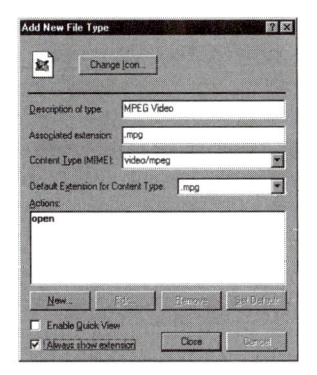

FIGURE 17.1 Configuring Internet Explorer for VMpeg 1.7.

5. Select the Close button to save this configuration and close the Add New File Type dialog box. To close the Options dialog box, select the Close button.

DISPLAYING MPEG FILES WITH INTERNET EXPLORER

The biggest problem in displaying MPEG files is waiting for them to download; some MPEG files can be several megabytes in size and can take half an hour or better to download. Now let's test the MPEG file type configuration you just made in Internet Explorer:

1. Open the File menu and choose Open. In the Open Location dialog box, enter the following URL:

   http://www.moran.com/falls/nfhome.html

2. Select the View of the Falls MPEG, 588k link to download this MPEG file. When the download is completed, Internet Explorer starts VMpeg 1.7 and the video (see Figure 17.2).

Lesson 17

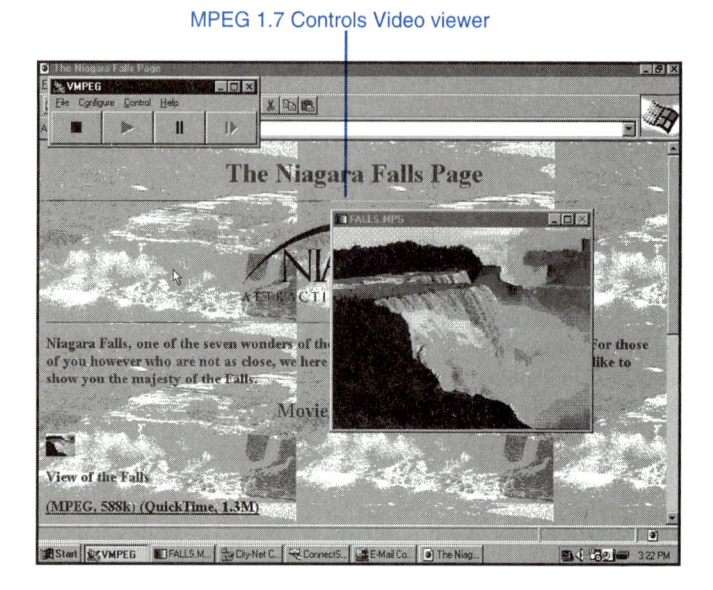

FIGURE 17.2 MPEG file displayed by Internet Explorer.

If you want to view other MPEG files, here are a couple of Web pages where you can find more:

- MPEG Movie Archive

    http://w3.eeb.ele.tue.nl/mpeg/index.html

- Kaleidospace

    http://www.kspace.com/

In this lesson, you learned about MPEG full-motion video files, including what application you need to display them, and how to configure Internet Explorer to display MPEG files. In the next lesson, you learn how to configure Netscape to use helper apps—its way of displaying other types of file formats.

LESSON 18

CONFIGURING HELPER APPS FOR NETSCAPE

In this lesson, you learn how to configure Netscape to use helper apps.

SETTING UP NETSCAPE TO USE HELPER APPS

In the previous lesson, you learned that Internet Explorer can't display every type of file format you encounter on the Web. Netscape has a similar display deficiency. To overcome this file display deficiency in Netscape, you have to set up what are called **helper apps**. Helper Apps are programs that enable Netscape to run or display files that Netscape can't display (or play) on its own.

> **Can't Play File!** If you try to play (or display) a file type that Netscape is not configured for, Netscape will display its Unknown File Type dialog box. This dialog box allows you to cancel the operation, save the file to disk, or configure a viewer for the file type. When you complete this lesson, you will know how to configure Netscape when you encounter an unknown file type.

Remember that when you configured Internet Explorer to work with other file types, the changes you made were not confined to Internet Explorer. The new file types you configured extended into the Windows 95 environment as file type associations similar to the file type associations that you created in Windows 3.1.

When you configure Netscape to use other file types, the configuration does *not* extend into the Windows 95 environment. The changes you make are confined to Netscape.

In the previous lesson, you configured Internet Explorer to play full-motion video files in the MPEG format. Another popular full-motion video format is the QuickTime format, which was developed by Apple Computers.

OBTAINING THE QUICKTIME VIEWER

Just as you went onto the Web to get an MPEG viewer for Internet Explorer, you'll also go onto the Web to find the QuickTime viewer that you'll use for Netscape:

1. Start Netscape. Open the File menu and choose Open Location. Enter the following URL in the Open Location dialog box to jump to the following Web page:

   http://quicktime.apple.com/

2. Scroll down to the **Download QuickTime** section and click the 2.0.3. for Windows link to download the QuickTime 2.0.3 viewer (see Figure 18.1).

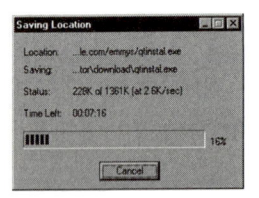

FIGURE 18.1 Downloading the QuickTime 2.0.3 viewer.

3. When the download is completed, use Windows Explorer to locate the downloaded file, qtinstal.exe. Double-click qtinstal.exe to install the QuickTime viewer (see Figure 18.2).

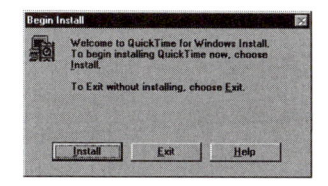

FIGURE 18.2 Installing QuickTime 2.0.3 viewer.

Configuring Netscape To Use QuickTime

Before Netscape can use QuickTime to display full-motion video, you must configure it to use a helper app. To configure Netscape to use QuickTime:

1. Open the Options menu and choose Preferences. Select the Helper Apps tab in the Preferences dialog box.

2. Select video/quicktime in the File Type list. For the Action option, select the Launch the Application radio button.

3. In the field under **Launch the Application**, enter the drive and path location where QuickTime 2.0.3 is installed, **C:\WINDOWS\Player.exe** (see Figure 18.3).

4. Choose OK. Now open the Options menu and choose Save Options to save the configuration.

Displaying QuickTime Movies with Netscape

Now that you've configured Netscape to play QuickTime movies, it's time to test your configuration.

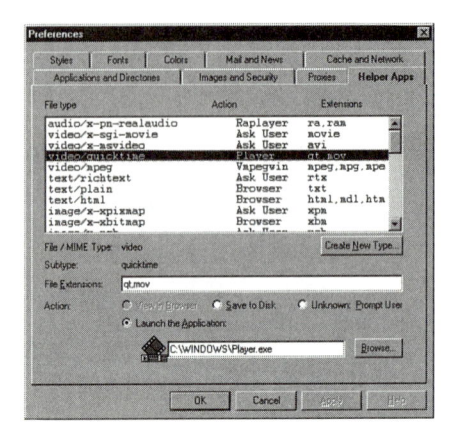

FIGURE 18.3 Configuring Netscape to use QuickTime 2.0.3.

1. Open the File menu and choose Open Location. Enter the following URL in the Open Location dialog box:

   http://tausq.resnet.cornell.edu/mmedia.htm

2. Scroll down to the titled section of the Web page, **Clips from Preview—Star Trek—Generations** and select the Part 1 link to download a QuickTime movie. This file takes about eight minutes to download if you have a 28.8 kbps Internet connection. When the download is completed, Netscape starts QuickTime 1.1 with the file stgen01.mov loaded. Select the Play button (shaped like a triangle pointing to the right) to start the preview of the movie *Star Trek: Generations* (see Figure 18.4).

> **TIP** **Where Are the Movies?** Whenever you download a file to be used with a Netscape helper app, the file is stored in the Windows \temp folder. If you download a file you want to keep, it's probably a good idea to move it to another folder.

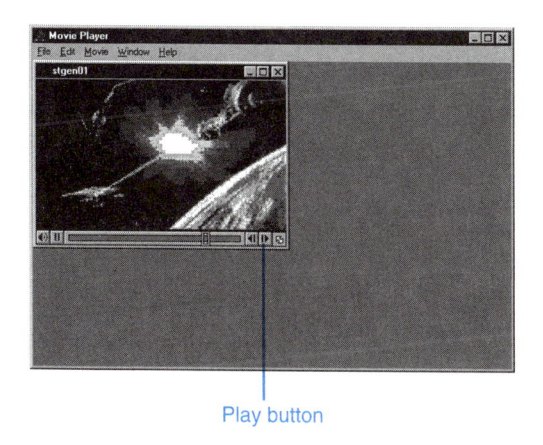

FIGURE 18.4 Preview of *Star Trek: Generations.*

An added bonus of QuickTime movies is the high-quality sound you'll hear if you have a sound card installed in your PC.

You can download other QuickTime movies from this page. If you're interested in viewing more QuickTime movies, be sure to visit these sites:

- **http://deathstar.rutgers.edu/people/bochkay/ movies.html**
- **http://w3.one.net/~flypba/ movie.trailer.index.html**

You can also locate QuickTime movie sites by searching for **quicktime movie** on Yahoo (**http://www.yahoo.com**).

Besides normal QuickTime movies, there is also a graphic file format called **QuickTime VR**, or **QuickTime Virtual Reality**. It could easily take another *10 Minute Guide* to explain QuickTime VR, but if you want to discover more about QuickTime VR on your own, the following Web site should be able to explain the basics and get you started:

http://qtvr.quicktime.apple.com/

In this lesson, you learned how to configure Netscape to display QuickTime movies. In the next lesson, you learn about Internet newsgroups and UseNet.

How UseNet Newsgroups Work

LESSON 19

In this lesson, you learn how UseNet newsgroups operate.

What Are UseNet Newsgroups?

UseNet newsgroups are nothing more than electronic discussion groups. In newsgroups, members usually limit their discussion to a single topic per group. More than 18,000 newsgroups exist and topics range from aviation and alien visits to Zen and zoology.

> **UseNet** The term "UseNet" actually predates the Internet. UseNet refers to an early system of connecting mainframe computers to one another using ordinary telephone lines and crude versions of desktop modems to transmit and exchange research discussion articles.

Even though newsgroups are, by definition, oriented to single topics, as you browse through newsgroups, you'll notice that a single article in a topic can take many sides, or **threads**. Threads result from other users posting replies to the original article, and even the original author responding to some of the discussion on the original topic. Some newsreaders make it easy to follow threads, but be warned: Threads have a way of veering off the original article's subject. As a rule, don't worry too much about following threads to the final reply.

> **Threads** Threads are the continuation of a newsgroup article and its accompanying discussion articles. The "thread" ties together the discussion articles.

Newsgroup members post messages that express their ideas and comments on the newsgroup topic. In most cases, newsgroups are neither censored nor moderated, but occasionally you will see a newsgroup where the administrator maintains a fairly strict policy concerning admittance of articles that do not directly pertain to the newsgroup subject. In these cases, the administrator deletes articles that aren't relevant to the discussion.

Members read and write additional messages about topics posted—either adding additional information, or arguing with (or for that matter, agreeing with) the author of the original message. Posted messages may only remain in the newsgroup a few weeks, mainly because they occupy storage space. Newsgroups are, in fact, managed by your service provider, who may not want to tie up storage space longer than a few weeks. It is also up to your service provider to carry newsgroups. This explains why an Internet user in Portland, Oregon may not have access to the same newsgroups as a user in Annapolis, Maryland. If you hear of a newsgroup that is not carried by your provider, all you may need to do is simply ask the provider to add that group.

How Newsgroups Are Organized

Newsgroups are organized into seven major categories:

- **alt** (alternative)—topics that fall outside of mainstream ideas and views; some can be very controversial

- **comp** (computers)—topics associated with computers and computer science

- **news** (newsgroups)—news about newsgroups and their operation

- **rec** (recreational)—topics that pertain to recreational interests
- **sci** (science)—topics or areas of scientific interest
- **soc** (social)—topics or areas pertaining to social issues
- **talk**—focuses on the aspects of a public debating forum

In addition to these seven major categories, many news servers also maintain a number of minor groups such as:

- **biz** (business)—business-related topics
- **bionet** (biology)—issues and ideas centered around biology and the biological sciences
- **courts**—court-related issues and events
- **general**—general interest topics not falling into any of the other groups
- **misc.** (miscellaneous)—sometimes just included to catch the overflow from general
- **humor**—humor, jokes, comedians, and so on.

You can encounter countless other newsgroups. If you're inclined to want to make your ideas heard (or at least read), you should have no problem finding a forum in which to express your views.

What You Need

If you're using Netscape as your browser, all you need is some basic information from your service provider because Netscape has some basic newsreader functions built-in. You need to know the names of your **news server** and your **mail server**. If you're not using Netscape, or if you want more functions than Netscape offers, you need a newsreader program. The next lesson explains which ones are good and where you can get them.

> **News Server** A news server is a file server provided by your Internet Service Provider. When you read newsgroup articles, you are reading them because they are supplied by your provider on a server that your provider maintains.

> **Newsreader** A newsreader is simply a program you use to read and post articles to a newsgroup.

What You See

For now, let's take a look at a sample newsgroup. Figure 19.1 shows the **alt** newsgroup listing as it appears in one of the newsreaders that's discussed in the next lesson, Free Agent.

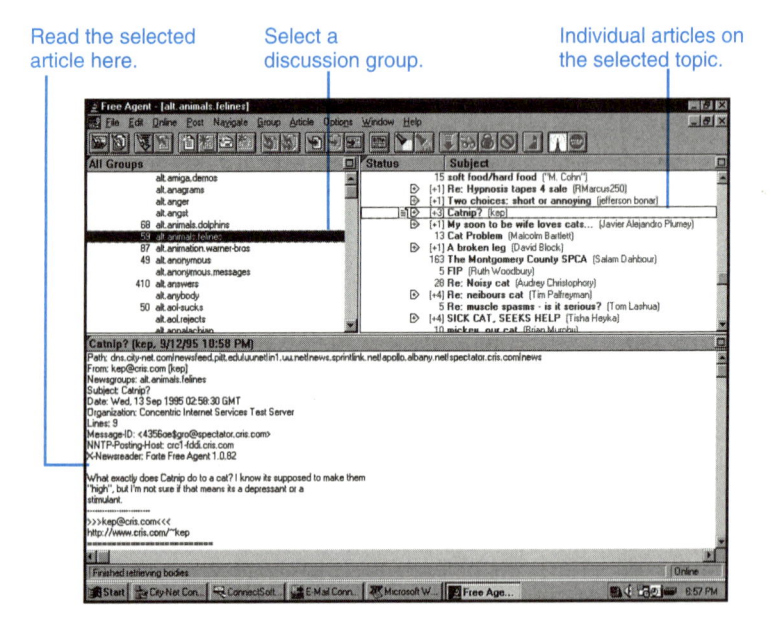

Read the selected article here.   Select a discussion group.   Individual articles on the selected topic.

Figure 19.1 alt newsgroup.

How UseNet Newsgroups Work 127

Many newsreaders show something similar to Figure 19.1. They show a list of available newsgroups, shown here in the upper-left corner of the screen. When you select a particular newsgroup, the newsreader shows you the current list of articles (and the number of articles currently in that newsgroup) or postings in that group, shown here in the upper-right corner of the screen. And when you select a message to read, the newsreader displays that message; this newsreader displays the message in the bottom half of the screen.

In this lesson, you learned about newsgroups, how they are organized and run, and what you can expect to see when you use them. In the next lesson, you learn how to set up and use newsreaders.

Lesson 20: Setting Up and Using a Newsreader

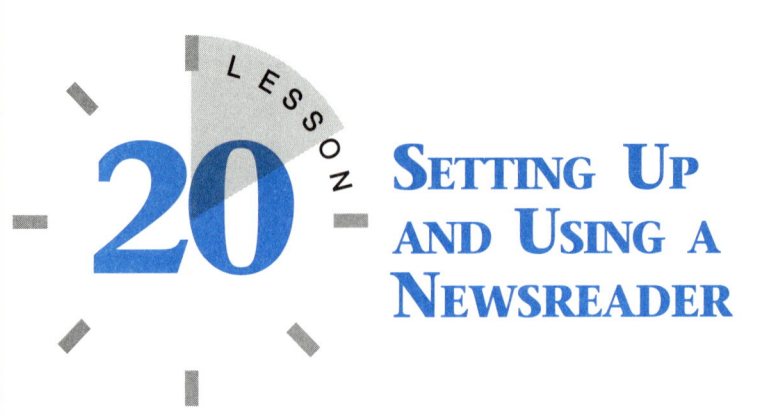

In this lesson, you learn how to set up and use a newsreader to read newsgroup postings on the Internet.

Acquiring and Setting Up Your Newsreader

If you're using Netscape as your browser, you can use its built-in, but rudimentary, newsreader capabilities. If you're serious about getting involved with UseNet newsgroups, however, you should use a full-functioned newsreader. You can download a number of good ones from the Internet.

Free Agent is gaining in popularity and has all the features you're likely to need or want for maintaining the articles of the newsgroups you subscribe to, for better control of keeping track of the articles you read and the articles you post. To download a copy:

1. Start your Web browser and jump to the following URL:

    http://www.forteinc.com/forte/

    This URL takes you to Forte's home page; Forte is the manufacturer of Free Agent (see Figure 20.1).

2. Follow the instructions and prompts to download Free Agent from the **Internet Products** area (see Figure 20.2).

Setting Up and Using a Newsreader 129

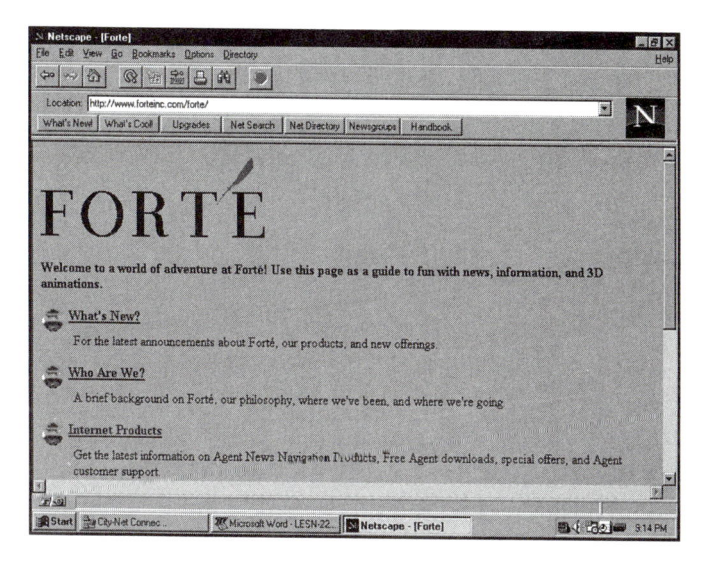

FIGURE 20.1 Forte's home page.

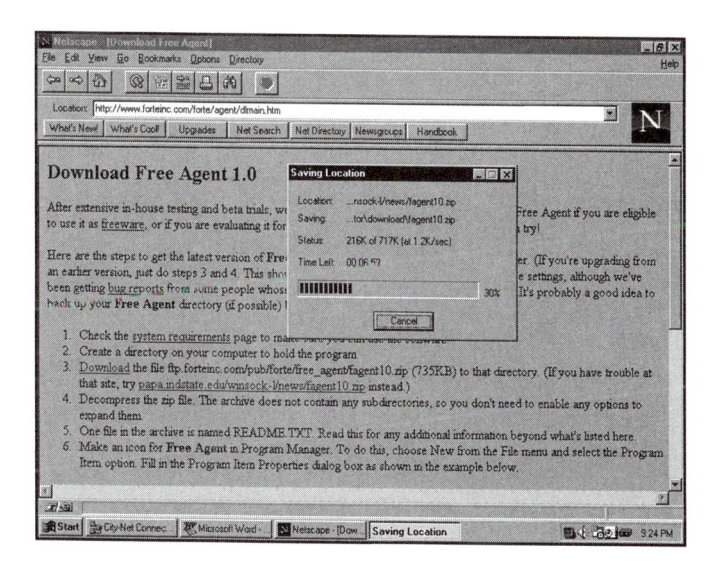

FIGURE 20.2 Downloading the Free Agent archive file.

> **TIP** **You Can Download Directly** If you would rather use your FTP utility, you can download the file fagent10.zip from one of two FTP sites: **ftp.fortinc.com/pub/forte/ free_agent/fagent10.zip** or **papa.indstate.edu/ winsock-1/news/fagent10.zip**.

3. Use WinZip or compatible unzipper to extract the contents of the downloaded archive file. Create a Windows shortcut to the Free Agent executable file AGENT.EXE so you can start it from your Windows start menu.

4. Double-click the Free Agent shortcut icon to start Free Agent. When the program starts, it asks you to accept the license agreement. Read the agreement, and then select the Accept button. Free Agent then prompts you to configure it to use your news server, mail server, your email address, your name (optional), and your time zone (see Figure 20.3). You can get the names of the news server and the mail server from your service provider. Choose OK to save the information you enter.

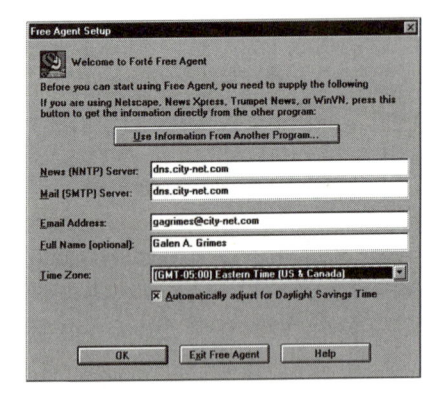

FIGURE 20.3 Configuring Free Agent.

> **TIP** — **Configure from Netscape** If you're using Netscape, and you were industrious enough (and ingenious enough) to enter news and mail information, you can transfer this information automatically to Free Agent by selecting the Use Information From Another Program button.

Reading News Articles

Once you've configured your newsreader, it automatically attempts to connect to your news server to start getting newsgroup information:

1. Free Agent attempts to go online to connect to your news server to get a complete listing of all newsgroups (see Figure 20.4). Choose Yes to allow Free Agent to go online to get the complete listing of your news server's newsgroups. This takes anywhere from a few minutes to a half an hour or more depending on the speed of your Internet connection.

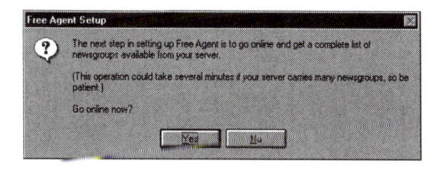

Figure 20.4 Free agent prompting you to get newsgroups.

2. When Free Agent displays the list of newsgroups it found on your news server, select a newsgroup that interests you and double-click. The View Empty Group dialog box appears (see Figure 20.5).

3. To view all articles your news server has on this newsgroup, select the Get All Article Headers button. Keep in mind that some active newsgroups can have several hundred or even several thousand articles; displaying

that many articles will take a few minutes. If you prefer to just see a sampling of the articles available under a group, select the Sample 50 Article Headers button. After the articles are retrieved, they are displayed as you see in Figure 20.6.

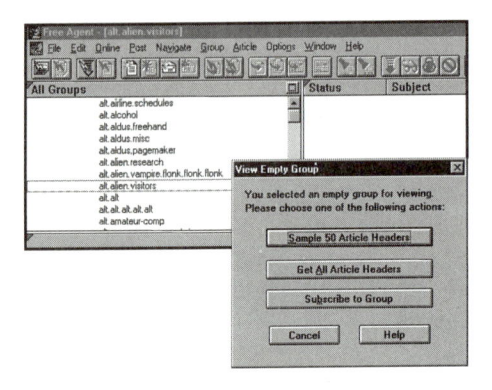

FIGURE 20.5 View Empty Group window.

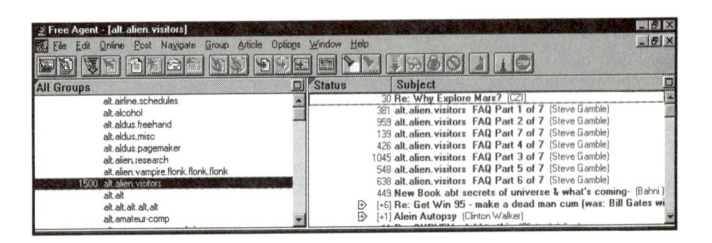

FIGURE 20.6 Articles displayed for selected newsgroup.

4. To read an article, select its header (title) and double-click it. The article you clicked appears (see Figure 20.7).

5. To read the threads (go back to lesson 19 if you don't remember what a thread is) associated with this article, select the View Next Unread Article in Thread icon. This displays the associated articles in the thread (see Figure 20.8).

Setting Up and Using a Newsreader 133

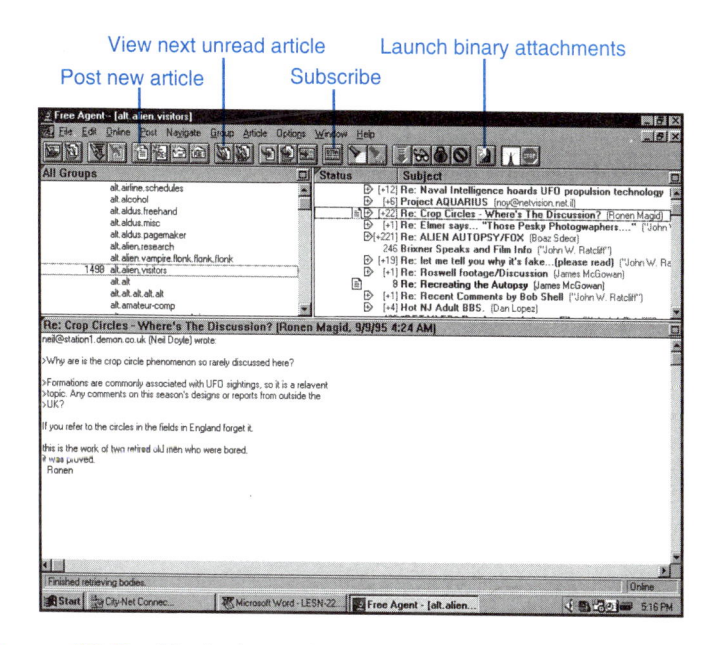

FIGURE 20.7 Displaying article.

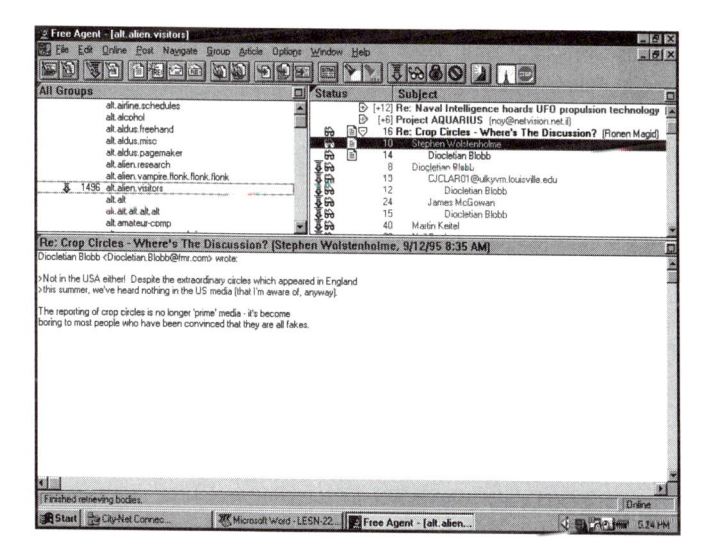

FIGURE 20.8 Associated articles in thread.

> **Identifying Icons** To identify the icons in the Free Agent toolbar, use your mouse to place the pointer on one of the icons, but don't click. The icon's name is displayed.

In this lesson, you learned how to configure a newsreader and use it to read articles in a newsgroup. In the next lesson, you learn how to subscribe to a newsgroup and post your own articles.

LESSON 21

SUBSCRIBING AND POSTING TO A NEWSGROUP

In this lesson, you learn how to subscribe to a newsgroup and how to post articles to it.

SUBSCRIBING TO A NEWSGROUP

In the last lesson, you learned how to set up a popular newsreader, Free Agent, and how to use it to read newsgroup articles. Now you'll see how to use your newsreader to subscribe to newsgroups that interest you and to post articles to them.

If you haven't already, go ahead and click the Free Agent icon on the Windows Start menu and start your newsreader. You don't have to subscribe to a newsgroup to read its articles or to post messages to it, but subscribing to newsgroups does have a few advantages. One major advantage is that you can set up your newsreader to display only the newsgroups you've subscribed to, as opposed to displaying the several hundred newsgroups carried by most news servers.

To subscribe to a newsgroup:

1. Scroll through the list of newsgroups found on your news server.

2. When you locate a newsgroup that interests you, click the group to highlight it and choose Group, Subscribe from the Free Agent menu bar. This procedure places a small newspaper icon next to the newsgroup (see Figure 21.1).

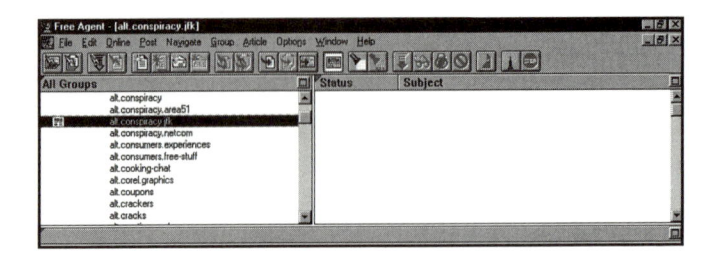

FIGURE 21.1 Subscribed-to group with icon.

> **Another Way To Subscribe** Here's a slightly faster way to subscribe: Highlight the group and then press Ctrl+S. You can also subscribe to a newsgroup by highlighting it and then by clicking the Subscribe icon.

To unsubscribe to a group, repeat the same action. This removes the icon and unsubscribes you from that newsgroup.

Displaying Only Subscribed-to Groups

After you select all the groups you find interesting, you can adjust your newsreader to display only those groups. By displaying only the groups you subscribe to, you can select and update the articles in those groups without the tedium of scrolling through several hundred newsgroups.

To display just the groups you subscribe to From the Free Agent menu bar, choose Group, Show Only Subscribed Groups. This sequence displays only the groups you've subscribed to (see Figure 21.2).

Posting a Newsgroup Article

Reading the articles posted on the newsgroups you've subscribed to is only half the fun of being a newsgroup junkie. To fully

Subscribing and Posting to a Newsgroup 137

appreciate the value of newsgroups, you have to **post** articles. Posting involves either responding to someone else's article or posting your own ideas.

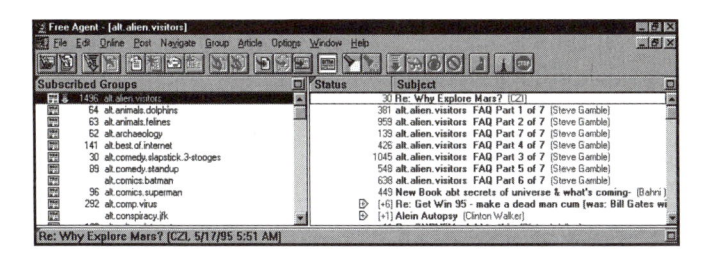

FIGURE 21.2 Free Agent displaying only subscribed-to groups.

> **Post** To post an article means simply to place an article that you write into the newsgroup for other users to read.

While you're getting started, I suggest that you stay away from the more "controversial" newsgroups, such as any involving sex, politics, or Kennedy assassination theories. Until you feel comfortable posting articles or responding to posted articles, try a few of the less controversial groups, such as rec.arts.disney-parks or alt.tv.game-shows.

> **I'm Getting Hate Mail!** Sooner or later you will post an article that someone will absolutely disagree with, and they'll ask you if your brains are at the end of your digestive tract. This is called a **flame**. And if you post a completely off-the-wall comment, expect to get lots of flames. This is how newsgroup subscribers vehemently disagree.

1. Select a newsgroup on your news server and display the articles under it contained on your news server.

2. Select an article title that you know something about or can make a comment on.

3. Open the article so that you can read it and so that your follow up (response) is properly formatted as a thread to the article. Then open the Post menu and choose Follow Up Article. When the follow up window appears, enter your response under the article to which you are responding (see Figure 21.3).

> **Follow up** Follow up articles are also referred to as reader comments.

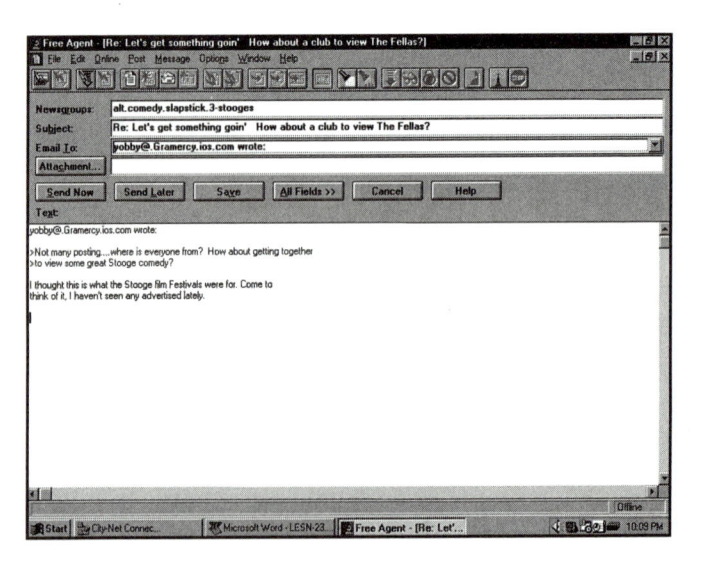

FIGURE 21.3 Follow up to a posted article.

4. When you finish, select the Send Now (or Send Later) button.

If you want to post a new article rather than respond to something written by someone else, open the Post menu (see step 3) and choose New Article.

The first few postings you do might seem a bit strange or awkward. After all, you're commenting on something created by a nameless and faceless entity.

> **TIP**
>
> **Know Your Netiquette** While newsgroups are designed to promote the free discussion of ideas and issues, newsgroups are not a free-for-all, no-holds-barred, public soapbox. There are rules of behavior that you must follow, or risk being excluded from newsgroups. Most of these concern personal attacks, and the use of obscene and racist language in postings. For a complete listing of Netiquette guidelines, go to the newsgroup news.announce.newusers and read (or better yet download) the article "Emily Postnews Answers Your Questions on Netiquette."

In this lesson, you learned how to subscribe to newsgroups and how to post articles. In the next lesson, you learn how to download and decode/encode newsgroup graphic files.

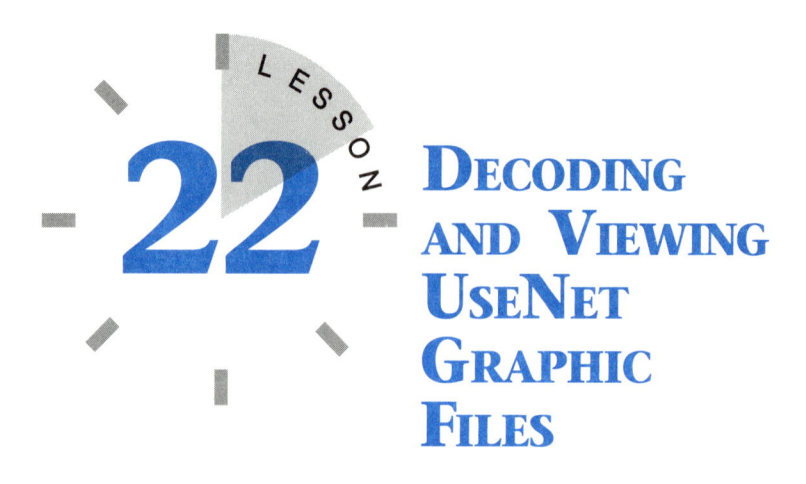

Lesson 22: Decoding and Viewing UseNet Graphic Files

In this lesson, you learn how to encode and decode UseNet graphic files.

UseNet Graphic Files

In addition to finding posted articles on newsgroups, you can occasionally find graphic files that a newsgroup member has posted to share with other users. Sometimes members post the file along with an article to help illustrate the point being made.

UseNet, however, is set up as a **text-based system**, which means that graphic files and pictures aren't readily accepted in binary form. To solve this problem, the early pioneers of UseNet developed a system of encoding and decoding binary files (graphic images, pictures, and executable programs) into text files. This encoding and decoding system is still often referred to as **UUencoding** and **UUdecoding**. The names come from UUCP, which stands for UNIX-to-UNIX Communications Protocol, an early means of transferring binary files from one UNIX computer system to another UNIX computer system.

The vast majority of the binary files you find in UseNet are graphics (usually pictures of people). You can also find sound files, archived ZIP files, and executable programs.

DECODING AND VIEWING USENET GRAPHIC FILES   141

> **Binary File**   Binary files are most often thought of as executable program files that contain instructions and commands for your computer. But in this example, binary files refer to any file that contains any characters that are not pure text. This includes graphic files and word processing document files that contain formatting and printing instruction codes.

> **ASCII**   ASCII, which stands for the American Standard Code for Information Interchange, is a means of creating pure text characters that are readable by all computers.

DECODING BINARY FILES

If you downloaded Free Agent back in Lesson 20, "Setting Up and Using a Newsreader," you already have the means to decode binary files you find in newsgroups:

> **Some Pictures May Offend!**   Be forewarned: Many, but not all, graphics in newsgroup binary files, are of nude or semi-nude people. Many of these files provide some advanced notice of the content of the picture, but this notice is neither a rule nor a prerequisite.

1. Locate and select an article that has a binary file attachment, or find a graphic file listed as an article. A clue that'll help you find graphic files is to look for the extensions GIF and JPG. Searching this way is probably easiest if your news server has a category called **alt.bin.** or **alt.binary.** (see Figure 22.1).

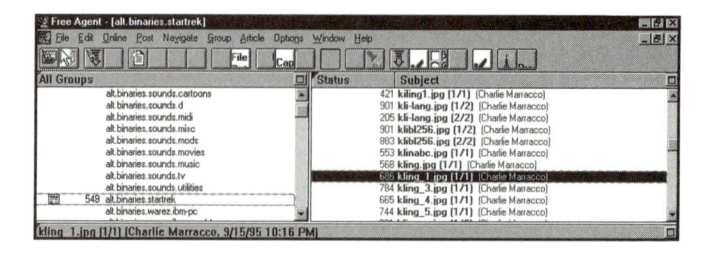

FIGURE 22.1   alt.binary. category on my news server.

2. Press Enter to retrieve the file. Depending on the size of the file and the speed of your connection, retrieving (downloading) the file can take anywhere from a few seconds to a few minutes.

3. When the retrieval (download) is complete, open the File menu and choose Save Binary Attachment. Free Agent converts the text-based file to a binary file.

4. After Free Agent converts the file into a binary format, it then launches your file viewer for that particular format. Press Enter to start the file viewer (see Figure 22.2).

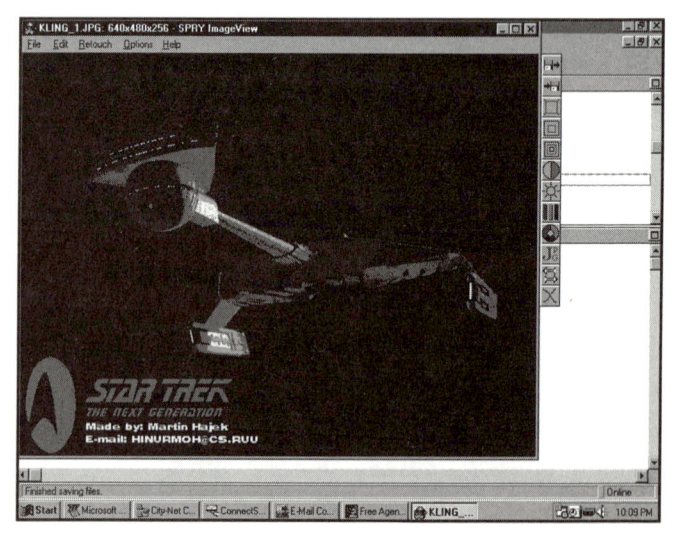

FIGURE 22.2   File viewer displaying retrieved file.

Decoding and Viewing UseNet Graphic Files 143

> **TIP** — **See the File Viewer** Windows 95 automatically configures a variety of graphic file viewers. On the off chance that you download a file that you can't view, you can often find instructions in the FAQ (Frequently Asked Questions) section of the newsgroup you're in or on your news server. You can also refer back to Lesson 17, "Adding File Types in MS Internet Explorer," to learn about locating and configuring file viewers for certain file types.

As with anything else new, you will probably have to try retrieving and decoding files a few times to get the hang of it, especially when file extensions do not readily identify their format. If you are curious as to what an encoded file looks like, trying reading an encoded file rather than downloading the file.

ENCODING BINARY FILES

Sooner or later, if you spend a lot of time in newsgroups, you will want to post a graphic file to share with other members.

Posting a binary file is a lot like posting a news article. You open the Post menu, decide whether it's a new article or a response to an existing article, write your message, attach the binary file, and then send your article.

To post a graphic file:

1. Create an article to post, the same as you did in Lesson 21, "Subscribing and Posting to a Newsgroup."

2. Select the Attachment button to locate (browse for) the binary file you want to attach to your message. As it posts the attachment, Free Agent automatically encodes the binary file into a text-based format.

In this lesson, you learned how to decode and encode UseNet graphic files. In the next lesson, you learn how to use an IRC chat program to communicate with other Internet users.

LESSON 23

REAL-TIME CHAT ON THE INTERNET

In this lesson, you learn about IRC, Internet Relay Chat, and how to set up and use a chat program.

WHAT IS INTERNET RELAY CHAT?

For some, **Internet Relay Chat**, or **IRC**, is the most enjoyable part of the Internet. As the name suggests, IRC is a means of "chatting" or having conversations with other Internet users in **real-time**. This means that both (all) of you are sitting down chatting at the same time. You aren't actually talking to the other users. You're conducting your conversation by typing your questions and responses. In turn, you see the questions and responses typed by other users in your chat group, or chat room.

To chat, you need an **IRC client**—which is the software needed to connect to an IRC server—and an **IRC server** to connect to. There are more than 100 IRC servers running on the Internet. We'll list a few at the end of this lesson.

IRC CLIENT SOFTWARE

You can download a number of good IRC client software programs from the Internet. Until recently though, they have all been text-based, and with good reason. If all you're doing to communicate with other users is typing, what good are pictures?

Well, one new IRC client program may be changing that way of thinking. A relatively new program called Worlds™ Chat has added a new dimension to Internet Relay Chat.

Worlds Chat takes place aboard an imaginary Space Station with a variety of rooms you can explore and chat in. Every person in Worlds Chat is represented by an Avatar, or Digital Actor. When you first enter Worlds Chat, you're given the opportunity to select an Avatar to represent the persona you want to present in the chat rooms. You can choose Avatars to represent both men and women in different age groups, ethnic and social status, and also choose from a variety of fictional characters. You also have to give your Avatar a name, which can be used to further enhance the persona you want to present.

> **Aliases Abound!** One important point worth driving home is that the names participants use in chat rooms can (and often do) change from session to session. Also, men can use women's names and vice versa. So be on guard that all is not as it necessarily appears. This is one aspect of IRC that can be both intriguing and irritating.

Getting and Configuring Worlds Chat

To get your copy of Worlds Chat, use your browser to jump to the following URL:

> **http://www.worlds.net/products/wchat/index.html**

This is the home page of Worlds Chat (see Figure 23.1).

Follow the prompts to the link for downloading the client software (including filling out the questionnaire first).

> **This File Is Huge!** Make sure you have the time and disk space to download the client program. Even in its compressed form, it's around 3 megabytes in size and will take about an hour to download at 14.4 kbps.

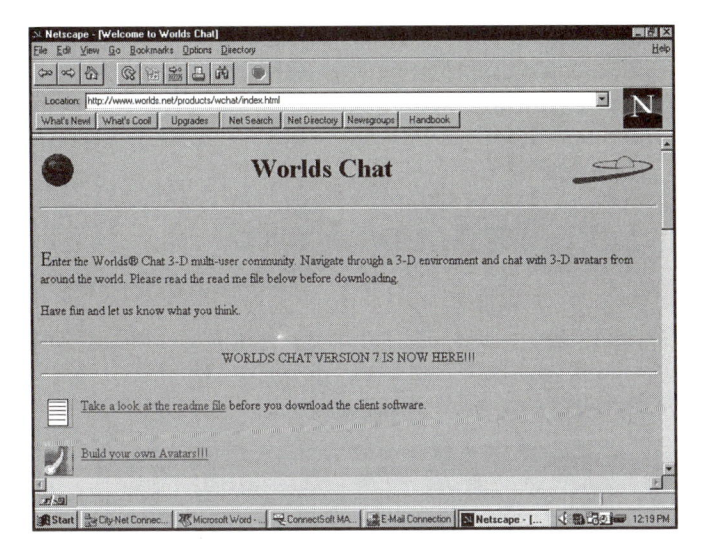

FIGURE 23.1 Worlds Chat home page.

To configure Worlds Chat:

1. Start the downloaded file, wchat07b.exe, as you would any other EXE file. The file wchat07b.exe is a self-decompressing archive file that is set up to unzip itself into the folder specified by your TEMP variable, or the current directory if no TEMP variable is used. After it's unzipped, it automatically launches its setup program to begin the installation and launch the Windows Program Manager (progman.exe)—yes, in case you didn't know it, Windows 95 does come with a Program Manager.

> **The File's Not There!** As we were testing Worlds Chat, it was still in beta testing (preliminary release of program). As it progresses through beta testing to finally become a finished product, the file name may change, but the Worlds Chat home page should have a link to the correct file name.

2. Follow the prompts to install Worlds Chat in the default folders, and accept the default installation suggestions. When you're done, you'll see the Worlds Chat shortcut on your Windows 95 menu.

Running Worlds Chat

Now that Worlds Chat is installed, you're ready to start it:

1. Double-click the Worlds Chat shortcut icon to start the program. Worlds Chat takes you to its Avatar Gallery where you can select your personality (see Figure 23.2).

Select an Avatar from the gallery posters

Figure 23.2 Worlds Chat Avatar Gallery.

2. To select an Avatar, use your mouse to browse through the gallery. Click the left mouse button to get a cursor, and then select an Avatar from one of the posters. When you select one to view, it's enlarged and starts to rotate so that you can see it from all sides (see Figure 23.3).

3. If you like the selected Avatar, select the Embody Me button, which is to the right of the Avatar. To look at more Avatars, select the Keep Looking button, which is to the left of the Avatar.

FIGURE 23.3 Viewing an Avatar.

4. After you select your Avatar, type in the name you want to use to identify your personality (see Figure 23.4). Notice that you can also choose to turn on music and sound.

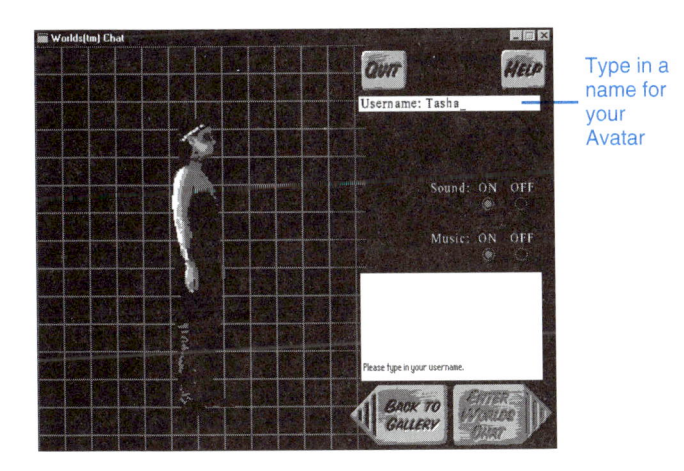

Type in a name for your Avatar

FIGURE 23.4 Naming your Avatar.

5. When you're ready to enter the Space Station, select the Enter Worlds Chat button.

LESSON 23

> **My Connection Timed Out!** If your Internet connection times out while connecting to the Worlds Chat server, it will still attempt to connect you, but in Single User mode. There's no fun in being the only person there. You basically just walk around an empty Space Station. Choose No and restart Worlds Chat.

6. When you first enter Worlds Chat, you're in the Hub Center (see Figure 23.5). Look at the map in the lower right-hand corner of your screen. See what looks like a square hub with six spheres extending from it? That's the Space Station. The square in the middle is the Hub Center and the spheres are different chat rooms. You can stay in the Hub Center, or move to a chat room. Click your mouse to get a cursor and then select one of the chat rooms by clicking one of the spheres.

Click here to see who's in the room with you.

3-D window allows movement using your mouse or arrow keys.

Chat text is here, currently in the small font.

Hub Center of the Space Station, surrounded by six spheres, each a different chat room

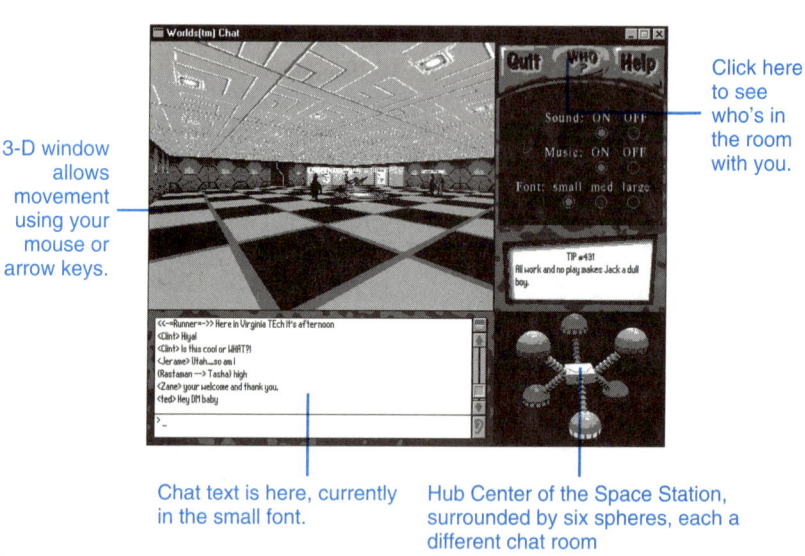

FIGURE 23.5 Space Station Hub Center.

7. When you enter a chat room, it's customary and polite to say hello to everyone. After that, you're free to join in on the conversation or just sit back and see how the talk is going. If you get bored, you can also go to another room to join in on other conversations. You can also set up private conversations with other users in the "tubes" connecting the chat rooms.

8. When you enter a new room, you can also select the Who? button in the upper right-hand corner to get a list of the people who are in the room with you.

> **TIP** **Read the Help Section!** Worlds Chat can be a bit daunting at first because there appears to be so much going on. Take a few minutes and browse through the Help section to help you get a better feel for how it all works. It will make your romp through Worlds Chat easier and a lot more enjoyable.

9. When you're ready to leave, simply select the Quit button and choose Yes to exit Worlds Chat.

Other IRC Client Programs

If Worlds Chat appears more involved than you want to get in IRC client software, you can download one of the "traditional" IRC client programs. One program that is fairly popular is WSIRC, which you can get from most FTP sites. In Gatekeeper, it's stored in the file wsircc20.zip in the directory /pub/micro/msdos/win3/winsock. WSIRC is a very good text-based IRC client program that comes with a detailed tutorial and a world-wide list of IRC servers. As you can see in Figure 23.6, WSIRC can be a lot busier than Worlds Chat.

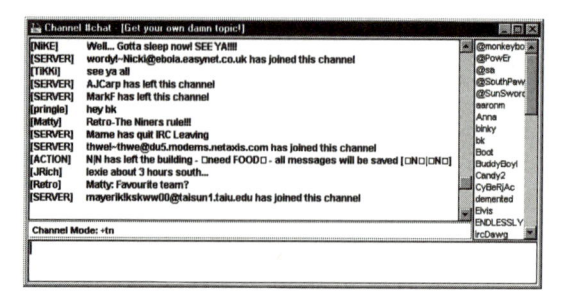

FIGURE 23.6 WSIRC displaying chat on the Telerama IRC server.

Here's a list of some IRC servers to visit:

- The Chat Server

  http://www.magmacom.com/~cbjustus/chatserver.html

- r.u.there?

  http://www.personalnet.com/

- Tulsa Chat

  http://tonyt.galstar.com/chat.htm

- Prospero's Global Stage

  http://www2.prospero.com/globalstage/

- Alumet Center for Education Online Service

  http://www.alumnet.com/

- The Disney Homepage

  http://www.umich.edu/~mingchen/disney.html

- Internet Relay Chat Information

  http://www2.undernet.org:8080/~cs93jtl/IRC.html

In this lesson, you learned about Internet Relay Chat (IRC) and about two different IRC client programs—Worlds Chat and WSIRC. In the next lesson, you learn about Gophers and Gopherspace.

LESSON 24: GOPHERING ON THE INTERNET

In this lesson, you learn about Gopher servers and how to access them using a Windows-based Gopher client program.

WHAT IS GOPHER?

In previous lessons, you learned about several specialized types of servers found on the Internet—FTP servers, Web servers, and news servers. Another type of server you're likely to encounter, especially if you ever use the Internet for conducting research, is a **Gopher server**. A Gopher server (or just **Gopher** for short) is similar in operation to an FTP server. This is because both are designed mainly as storage facilities; FTP servers mainly store programs and utility files, while Gopher servers mainly store document files. Gopher servers, however, have one main advantage over FTP servers in that Gopher servers have a highly organized menu structure.

Gophers originated at the University of Minnesota—the home of the Golden Gophers—hence the name.

This menu structure also interconnects one Gopher server with other Gophers much the same way that a Web page is linked to other Web pages. This interconnection of Gophers has been given the collective term **Gopherspace**.

USING A GOPHER CLIENT PROGRAM

Netscape has some limited Gopher client functionality built-in (as does Internet Explorer), but if you're seriously considering exploring the realm of Gopherspace, you should invest in a good Gopher client program. Many are available on the Internet in shareware form.

> **Gopher Client** A Gopher client is simply someone who uses a Gopher server—meaning you. A Gopher client program is merely the software you use to access a Gopher server.

Using HGopher

One of the better Gopher programs is HGopher, a public domain program written by Martyn Hampson. HGopher can usually be found on FTP servers in the hgoph24.zip file. The main FTP server where you can find it is **lister.cc.ic.ac.uk** in the /pub/wingopher directory. You can also find it at **gatekeeper.dec.com** in the /pub/micro/msdos/win3/winsock directory.

Installing HGopher

After you download hgopher.zip, here's how you install it:

1. Copy hgoph24.zip into its own folder, and use WinZip to decompress its archived contents into the Windows TEMP folder.

2. Create a shortcut to hgopher.exe so that you can start the program from your desktop menu.

Setting Up HGopher

After you install HGopher, you need to configure it before using it for the first time:

1. Make sure you're connected to your Internet provider.

2. Double-click the HGopher shortcut icon to start it. HGopher will start and display its default set of bookmarks (see Figure 24.1).

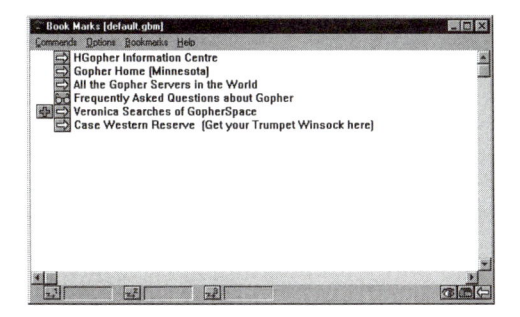

FIGURE 24.1 HGopher's main screen.

3. Open the Options menu and choose Gopher Set Up to open the Gopher Set Up Options dialog box (see Figure 24.2).

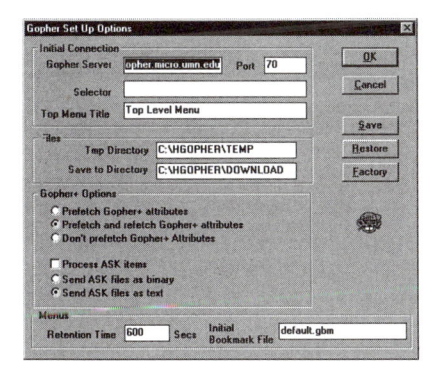

FIGURE 24.2 HGopher's Set Up Options dialog box.

4. Enter gopher.micro.umn.edu in the **Gopher Server** field. This takes you to the University of Minnesota's Gopher server.

5. If you want to save temporary files and downloaded files to different directories, enter the appropriate directories in the **Files** area of the dialog box.

> **TIP** — **Make Two Folders for Downloading** You might find it helpful to create two download folders here—one for downloading regular files, and one for downloading ZIP files that you will later have to unzip. Often, after installing a zipped file, there will be extra files that you can delete, which will be easier if they are in a separate folder.

6. Select the Save button to save your configuration settings. Choose OK to close the Gopher Set Up Options dialog box.

Searching Gopherspace

Now that you have HGopher configured, you're ready to begin your first Gopher search.

Gopher is set up to allow you to do two basic types of searches:

- You can search by stepping down through its various levels of menus.
- You can use its search engine to enter a query and allow Gopher to find the information you request.

Let's begin by first doing a hierarchical search. In this search, you will take a look at movie reviews for the year 1987:

1. At the HGopher main screen, double-click the Gopher Home (Minnesota) bookmark. In a few seconds, if the Gopher server has not reached its capacity (like other Internet servers, Gophers too have a maximum capacity for the number of users who can access it simultaneously), you will log in to the University of Minnesota Gopher (see Figure 24.3).

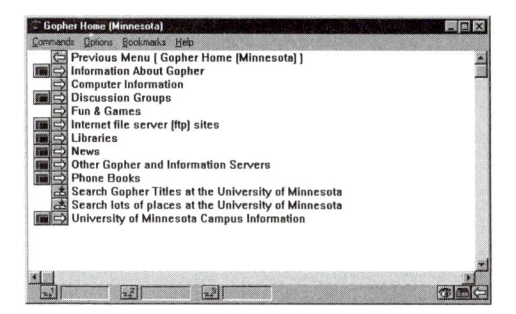

FIGURE 24.3   University of Minnesota Gopher.

2. At the main menu of the University of Minnesota Gopher, select Fun & Games by double-clicking that menu item. At the Fun & Games menu, select Movies. This takes you to the Movies menu, shown in Figure 24.4.

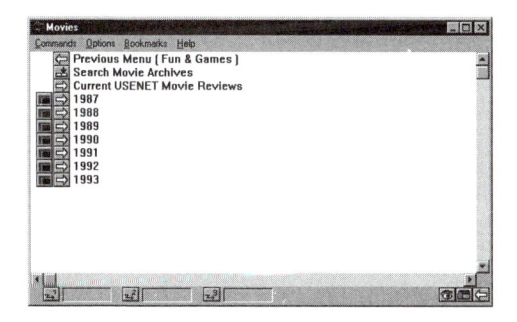

FIGURE 24.4   Gopher Movies menu.

3. To look at 1987 movies, select 1987. This selection gives you the breakdown for that year by month. You can now select any or all of the 12 months to review the listed movie reviews. If you select Apr, you'll get a listing of the movie reviews for that month. Select one of the movie reviews, such as *Lethal Weapon*, and you'll see that review (see Figure 24.5).

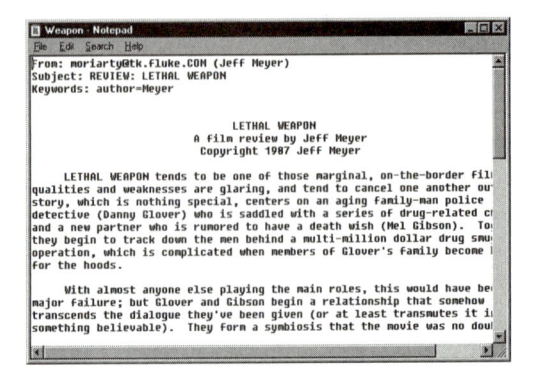

FIGURE 24.5 *Lethal Weapon* review.

Now let's conduct a search using the Gopher search engine:

1. Double-click the Search lots of places at the University of Minnesota menu item to conduct the widest possible search for the requested query. This opens the Index Search dialog box (see Figure 24.6).

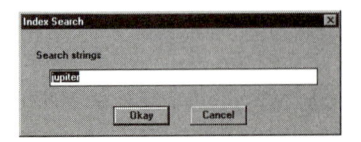

FIGURE 24.6 Index Search dialog box.

2. To search for information on jupiter, for example, enter jupiter in the **Search strings** field and choose Okay. In this case, case-sensitivity is not a problem, but with other Gopher programs it might be, so check the FAQ first.

3. Within a few seconds, the results of the search appear (see Figure 24.7).

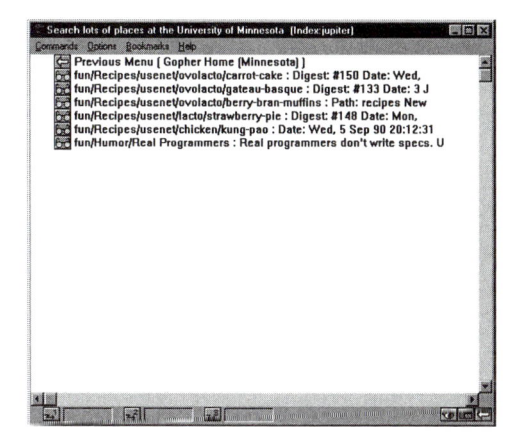

FIGURE 24.7 Results for the search on **jupiter.**

Obviously, there's a lot more to Gophers and Gopher searches than is covered here. However, you now know the basics of browsing through a Gopher server to search for additional information. Most of the Gophers you visit will have a menu item listing information about Gophers in general, or that Gopher in specific. This menu item is always a good place to start when looking for more detailed information. You should also pay attention to the icons that appear next to menu items. They will vary depending on which Gopher client program you're using, but if you pay attention, you should be able to detect which icons represent menus and menu items, which represent search engines, and which represent documents. When in doubt, check the Help section of the Gopher client or the FAQ.

In this lesson, you learned about Gophers and Gopher searches. In the next lesson, you learn how to conduct Veronica searches on Gophers.

LESSON 25
GOPHERING WITH VERONICA

In this lesson, you learn how to use Veronica for Gopher searches.

USING VERONICA TO DO GOPHER SEARCHES

In the last lesson, you used the Gopher client HGopher to conduct searches on the Gopher server at the University of Minnesota. These simplified searches were limited to that particular Gopher. What happens if the information you request is not located on the Gopher server you're searching? You can do an exhausting search, going from Gopher to Gopher, hoping to stumble across one that contains the information you're seeking—or you can use Veronica.

> **Why Veronica?** The name Veronica is an acronym for the name of the Gopher search system, **V**ery **E**asy **R**odent-**O**riented **N**et-wide **I**ndex to **C**omputerized **A**rchives. It's intended as a pun on the cartoon character "Archie," which is the name of one of the earliest FTP server search systems. Others believe that Archie was just a take-off of the word "archive."

Veronica is a Gopher search system. It's designed to periodically scan *all* Gopher servers everywhere, and to keep track of every title located on every Gopher server. The benefits of this type of search system should be immediately evident—Veronica does all

Gophering with Veronica 161

the work, and you get the benefit of those laborious searches through all of the Internet's Gopher systems.

If Veronica is included on the Gopher you're using, it's a service of the Gopher, and not a part of your client system. This means that you can conduct Veronica searches from just about any Gopher client to which you have access.

In the previous lesson, you may have noticed that there is a menu item on the University of Minnesota main screen titled **Other Gopher and Information Servers**. Double-click this menu item to conduct Veronica searches (see Figure 25.1).

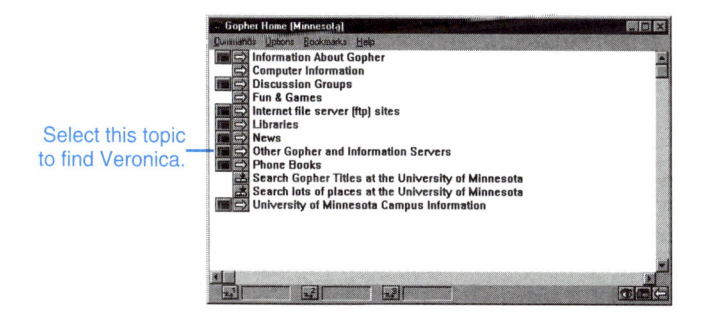

Select this topic to find Veronica.

Figure 25.1 Univ. of Minnesota's menu option for Veronica.

> **TIP** **Don't Select HGopher Veronica!** The bookmark that HGopher is configured to use for Veronica searches has been changed. The bookmark doesn't work. Use the menu selection for Veronica searches on the Univ. of Minnesota Gopher instead.

Double-click the Other Gopher and Information Servers menu item to go to the Veronica search menu (see Figure 25.2).

LESSON 25

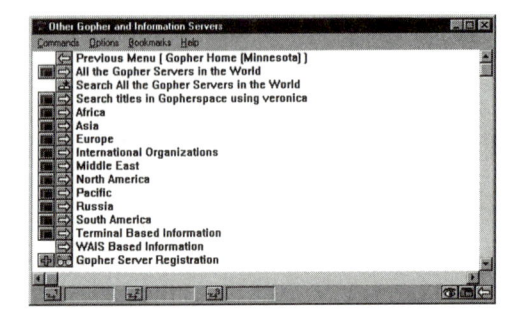

FIGURE 25.2 Univ. of Minnesota Veronica search menu.

Now you're ready to conduct a Veronica search:

1. Select the menu item Search titles in Gopherspace using veronica. This takes you to the menu shown in Figure 25.3.

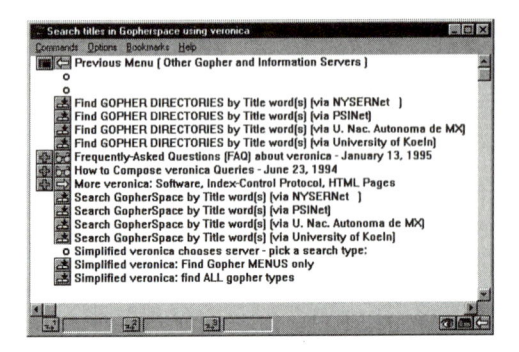

FIGURE 25.3 Univ. of Minnesota Veronica system.

2. To conduct a simple search, double-click the menu item Simplified veronica: Find Gopher MENUS only. The Index Search dialog box opens (see Figure 25.4). Enter **jupiter** as the search string. Choose Okay to begin the search.

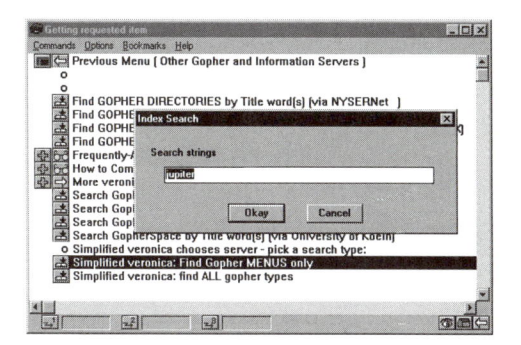

FIGURE 25.4 Index Search dialog box.

3. In a few minutes, the results of your search appear on-screen (see Figure 25.5).

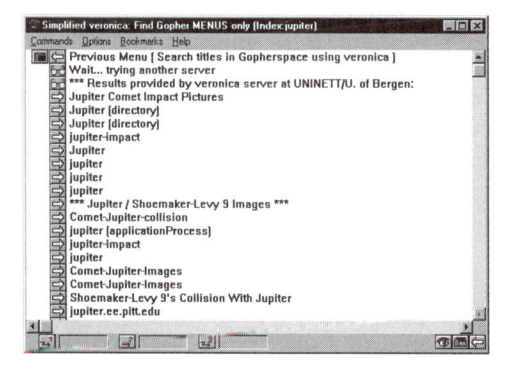

FIGURE 25.5 Veronica search results.

4. Double-click some of the menu items appearing in the results screen. Some will be directories on other Gophers leading to documents on the requested subject (see Figure 25.6), some will be documents, some will be graphic images, and some will be nothing. These are documents that have either been deleted or filed in a different location on the Gopher since the Veronica system performed its last scan on this Gopher.

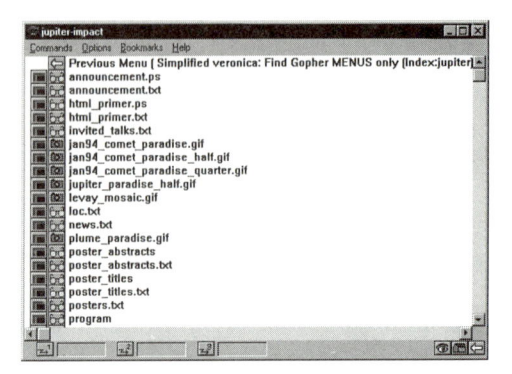

FIGURE 25.6 Directory containing documents and graphic images found during Veronica search.

Icon	Description
	Link to Gopher menu
	Text document in TXT format
	Text document in PostScript format
	Graphic file

This example was of a very simplistic Veronica search. Veronica searches can be more complex depending on what you want to search for and what parameters you want to set for your searches. We just scratched the surface of the Veronica system here. If you want more detailed information on performing Veronica searches, most Veronica systems have a document posted on their main menu that supplies information on how to perform complex searches, or has a Frequently Asked Questions (FAQ) document.

In this lesson, you learned how to use Veronica to conduct searches on multiple Gopher systems. In the next lesson, you learn how to telnet to Multi-User Dimensions (MUDs).

LESSON 26
TELNETTING TO MULTI-USER DOMAINS

In this lesson, you learn how to use the MS Telnet program to enter Multi-User Domains (MUDs).

MULTI-USER DOMAINS

Multi-User Domains, or **MUDs**, (also called **Multi-User Dimensions** and **Multi-User Dungeons**) are games that allow lots of users to participate simultaneously. If you remember the original Zork game series, then you have an idea how MUDs are played. MUDs and their cousins MOOs (MUDs Object Oriented), MUSHes, MUGs, and MUSEs (MUSHes, MUGs, and MUSEs are just derivations of MUDs), are text-based games in which you move around through an imaginary environment, examine objects and people you encounter, and solve various tasks to reach the end of the journey and solve the game's puzzle. MUDs are similar in operation to the old single-user, text-based Zork games, except that now numerous users play the game together. They are free to come and go within the environment of the game, and these users can "create" their own characters.

PLAYING A MUD

As mentioned earlier, to play a MUD, you need to use the Microsoft Telnet program that is part of Windows 95. Telnet is a text-based program that allows you to run a program on a remote computer. In this case, you're using Telnet to run a MUD. Here's an example of how it's done:

LESSON 26

1. Select the Start button on the taskbar and choose Run.
2. Type **telnet://guest@jhm.ccs.neu.edu:1709/** to jump to the JHM MOO (see Figure 26.1).

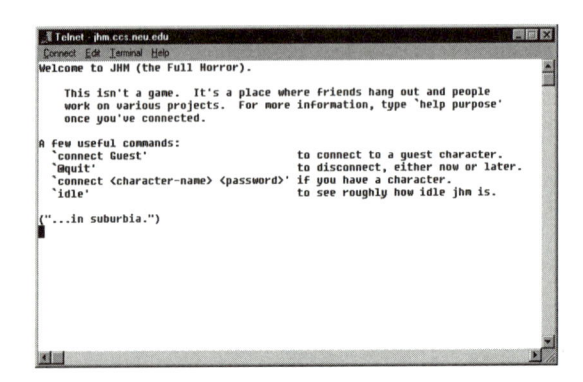

FIGURE 26.1   The JHM MOO through MS Telnet.

3. To continue, type **connect Guest** (see Figure 26.2).

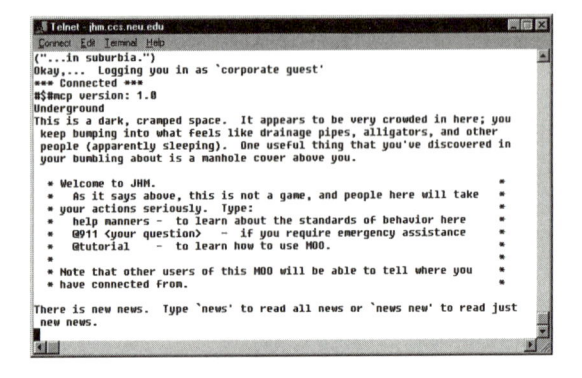

FIGURE 26.2   The JHM MOO continues.

> **TIP** — **What Am I Typing?** If you want to see what you're typing while using Telnet, open the Terminal menu and choose Preferences. Select the Local Echo check box. Now, whatever you type will "echo" back from the system you are logged in to and appear on your screen.

4. If you're interested in hanging around a while and want to learn more about this MOO, type **@tutorial** to run the tutorial program (see Figure 26.3).

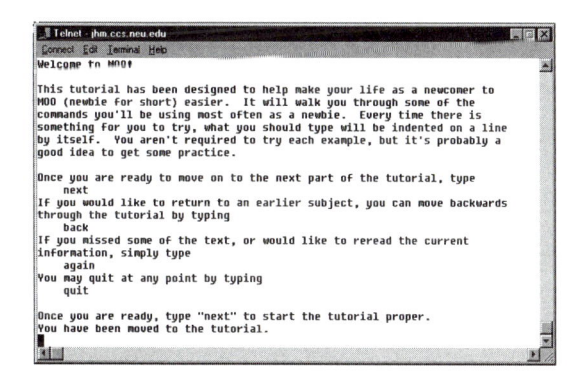

FIGURE 26.3 The JHM MOO tutorial.

If you're really interested in MUDs and MOOs, the only real problem you face is finding them. Fortunately, like most other resources on the Internet, they are fairly well-documented in most of the search engines like Yahoo and Lycos. One good place to start is at the University of Minnesota Gopher site you visited in Lesson 24.

1. Start HGopher and jump to the University of Minnesota Gopher.

2. Select the Fun & Games, Games, MUDs, Links to MUDs via Telnet link to get to the Gopher menu shown in Figure 26.4.

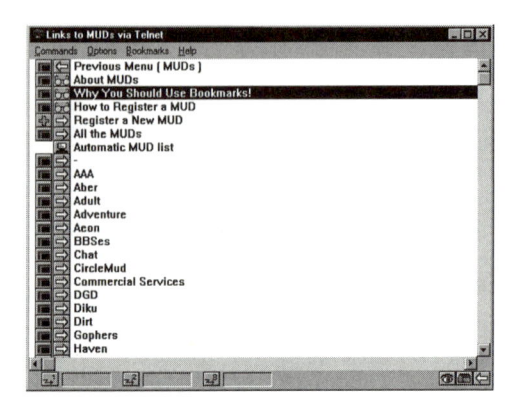

FIGURE 26.4 MUD listings on Univ. of Minnesota Gopher.

ADDING A NEW DIMENSION TO MULTI-DIMENSION

In an attempt to add a new dimension to MUDs, Chaco is producing a multimedia game extension to MUDs called Pueblo. Pueblo is supposed to supply graphics and visual references to MUDs and MOOs. Unfortunately, in the release we tested (version 0.90) it repeatedly crashed (itself, not Windows). If you would like to follow the progress of Pueblo until it is a stable and mature product, it can be downloaded from its Web site at:

   http://www.chaco.com/pueblo/

In this lesson, you learned how to use MS Telnet to access Multi-User Domain games. In the next lesson, you learn how to access the Internet through The Microsoft Network.

LESSON 27: Connecting Through the Microsoft Network

In this lesson, you learn how to access the Internet through The Microsoft Network.

What Is The Microsoft Network?

Microsoft officially launched The Microsoft Network (MSN) about the same time it released Windows 95. MSN is structured as an organized online service, similar in operation to other online services such as CompuServe, America Online, and Prodigy. All of these services are maintained and controlled by a parent organization. This control allows each online provider to structure the services each offers its clients. What this means to you, the user, is that the provider can always tell you how to find and access each service.

The Internet, on the other hand, is not controlled by a centralized entity. Users who want to set up their own Web server, FTP site, or Gopher can do so, at any time—or at any time discontinue their servers and sites without notifying anyone.

Look at it this way: Online services are like shopping malls, while the Internet is like a flea market—a very large flea market!

MSN, like other online services, offers files for downloading and support on hardware and software problems by various manufacturers. MSN also offers online financial advice, advice and information on hobbies and other pastimes, organized chat rooms, leisure and travel guides, electronic mail, and Internet access (see Figure 27.1).

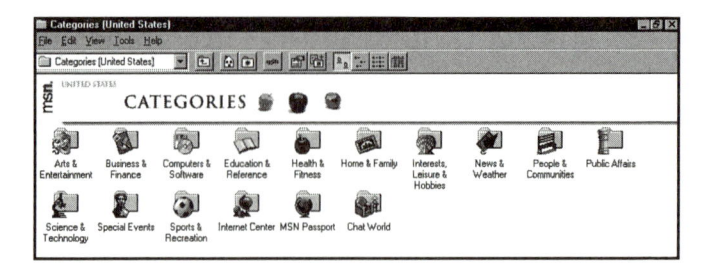

FIGURE 27.1 Some of the offerings on MSN.

Subscribing to MSN

Windows 95 contains all you need to subscribe to and access The Microsoft Network:

1. Double-click the MSN icon on your desktop and, if you haven't already signed on, MSN will prompt you throughout the sign-on process (see Figure 27.2).

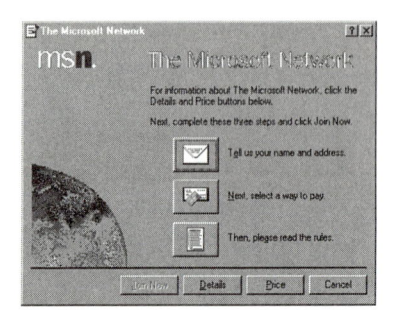

FIGURE 27.2 Subscribing to The Microsoft Network.

> **What MSN Icon?!** If the MSN icon doesn't appear on your desktop, you probably didn't install it when you installed Windows 95. Get out your Windows 95 disks or CD-ROM, and choose Start, Control Panel, and double-click the Add/Remove Programs icon to install MSN.

2. Follow the instructions on-screen. To access MSN, you will need to supply your name, address, phone number, and method of payment. You'll also need to select an ID and password. If you've gone through the previous 26 lessons (specifically Lessons 5, 6, and 7), your modem is already set up correctly. If you started with this lesson, make sure your modem is configured correctly.

3. Once you've completed the subscription setup, you're ready to log in. Double-click the MSN icon on your desktop, enter your ID and password, and, in a few seconds, you should see The Microsoft Network welcome screen (see Figure 27.3).

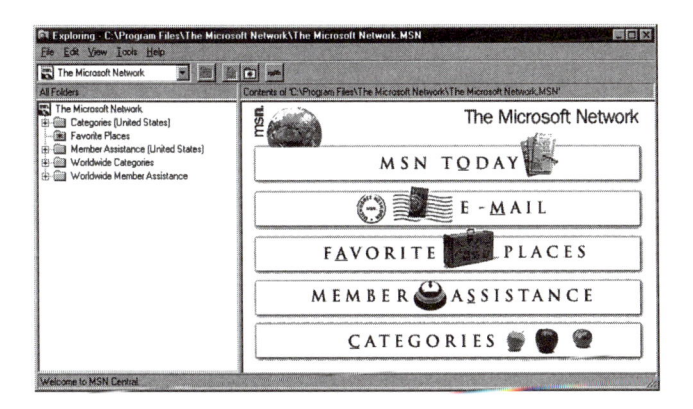

FIGURE 27.3 The Microsoft Network welcome screen.

4. A good place to start exploring is Categories. Click Categories to go to the Categories section (see Figure 27.4).

5. If you're interested in how you can access the Internet through MSN, select the Internet Center icon. You go to The Microsoft Network Internet Center (see Figure 27.5). Take some time to investigate the various options Microsoft provides here for Internet access. Also, notice the Internet Explorer icon; it's labeled **World Wide**

Web (WWW). It's the same Internet Explorer you used in earlier lessons; just click it to access the World Wide Web through MSN.

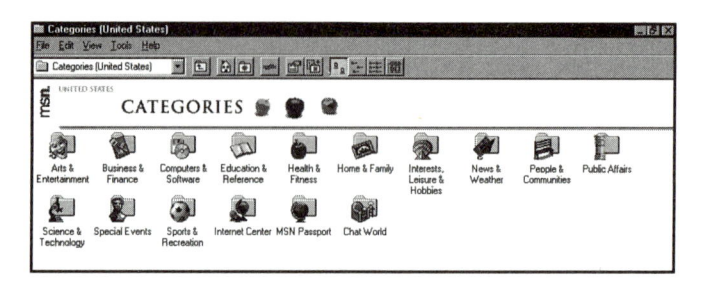

FIGURE 27.4 MSN Categories section.

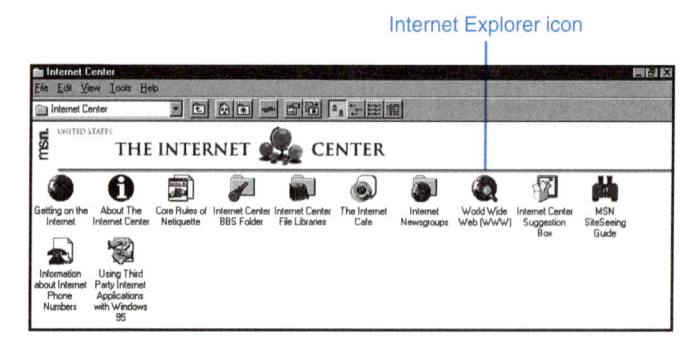

FIGURE 27.5 MSN's Internet Center.

Pros and Cons of Accessing the Internet Through MSN

By now, you're probably wondering what the pros and cons are of accessing the Internet through your service provider versus accessing the Internet through MSN.

If you access through MSN, your initial setup is a lot easier, you have access to all of the "extras" that Microsoft has provided in the Internet Center, plus you have access to the remaining

Connecting Through the Microsoft Network 173

features of the Microsoft Network—the ones you saw in the Categories section. These features are easily and conveniently arranged for you within the confines of MSN. You don't have to go searching for them like you would if you entered the Internet through your service provider.

The main disadvantage of using MSN as your Internet Provider is the cost. The standard MSN subscription cost is $4.95 per month, which provides up to 3 hours of connect time. Each additional hour costs you $2.50. Many Internet Service Providers charge a flat fee in the neighborhood of $20-30 per month. My service provider charges me $20 per month for unlimited access. However, according to my provider, this "unlimited access" may not last long. Soon, the charge may be $20 for the first 100 hours of connect time. If I accessed the Internet through MSN, under the standard plan, that same 100 hours would cost me $247.45 ($4.95 + (97 × $2.50) = $247.45). You can periodically check to make sure Microsoft does not change its online charges, but currently MSN and the other online services are all much more expensive than the vast majority of Internet Service Providers.

Granted, most users won't use 100 hours of connect time per month, but you can see that the charges do add up. Remember that while you're using MSN, the meter is running.

In this lesson, you learned how to sign on to The Microsoft Network. You also learned about some of the online services available on MSN, and how to access the Internet through MSN.

Congratulations! You are now an experienced Windows 95 Internet user. But don't put Que's *10 Minute Guide to the Internet with Windows 95* on the shelf yet. Keep it near your workstation to use as a quick reference whenever you have trouble remembering any of the commands and options covered in these lessons.

APPENDIX A

CREATING A SCRIPT FOR DIAL-UP NETWORKING

Another bonus that comes with the Microsoft Plus! add-on package is the ability to create an automated script for your Dial-Up Networking connection to your Internet Service Provider. Most providers give you a username or login ID—it's usually the first part of your email address. For example, my email address is *gagrimes@city-net.com*. The username given to me by my provider is *gagrimes*.

For example, when I dial up my provider, here's how I log in:

1. I wait for the prompt to enter my username. At the prompt, I enter my username, and then press the Enter key.

2. I wait for the prompt to enter my username password. At the prompt, I enter my password, and then press the Enter key.

3. I wait for the prompt to enter my connection type. At the prompt, I enter **PPP** for my connection type, and then press the Enter key.

I do all of these steps in the Terminal window, after my Dial-Up Networking connection has dialed my provider. But by creating a dial-up script, I can have all of these steps done automatically after dialing my provider.

CREATING YOUR DIAL-UP SCRIPT

The first thing you need to do is print out the document that describes the command language for Dial-Up scripting. The file is SCRIPT.DOC and it is located in your PLUS! folder.

> **TIP** — **I Can't Find SCRIPT.DOC!** If you're having trouble locating the file SCRIPT.DOC, use the Windows 95 Find utility. Open the Start menu and choose Find, Files or Folders. The Find All Files dialog box appears with the Name & Location tab selected by default. Enter **SCRIPT.DOC** in the **Named** field.

Read through the document, but don't be overwhelmed by the command language used in the scripting language. Most likely, you only need to use three or four commands. I did my script using only two commands—**waitfor** and **transmit**.

Here's how to create your script:

1. Log in to your provider just as you normally do. Make a written list of every action you take and every prompt you see in the Terminal window. Make sure that when you write down the prompts, you write down exactly what you see. Distinguish between upper- and lowercase letters.

2. Look for the commands in the command list (in SCRIPT.DOC) that seem to correspond to the actions taken when you log in. In my example, I **waitfor** a series of separate prompts, and then I **transmit** a response.

3. Use a text editor to write your script file. Remember, the first command in the script must be **proc main** and the last command must be **endproc**. All the commands you enter go between these commands. Keep your script very basic to begin with. If the first action is to wait until you are prompted to enter your username, you'll enter something like:

waitfor "Enter username:"

Don't forget to enclose the prompt in quotes.

> **Don't Use WordPad!** You might be tempted to use the WordPad editor that comes with Windows 95. Don't! WordPad will not create a pure text file. WordPad will include formatting and printing codes in your document that will cause errors in the script. Use Notepad instead.

4. To enter your response as a command, such as to respond with your username, you'll enter something like:

   transmit $USERID, raw

   This command will respond to the previous prompt with the username you entered in the Internet Setup Wizard (you might want to refer to Lesson 6). Normally, after you enter your username, you press the Enter key. To "press" the Enter key after transmitting your user ID, enter the command:

   transmit "<cr><lf>"

   Don't forget the quotes.

> **The Enter Key** When you press the Enter key, two characters are actually sent as that one keystroke. The Enter key's function originates from the days of manual typewriters when you had to manually hit the carriage return lever, and a "line feed" was included that advanced the paper up one line so you could begin typing on a new line.

5. If your login procedure with your provider is simple, you can just continue to enter a series of **waitfor** and **transmit** commands.

6. After you finish writing your script, save the file with the extension SCP in your Accessories folder (which should be C:\Program Files\Accessories, unless you changed it).

The next step is to assign the script file to your Dial-Up Networking connection:

1. Select the Start button on the taskbar and choose Programs, Accessories, Dial-Up Scripting Tool to start the Dial-Up Scripting Tool.

2. In the Dial-Up Scripting Tool dialog box, enter the name of your script file in the **File name** field. If you placed your script file in the Accessories folder, you do not need to include the drive and path with the file name.

3. Make sure that neither of the check boxes (**Step through script** and **Start terminal screen minimized**) is selected.

4. In the Connections list, highlight the name of the connection you use for your provider. Select the Apply button; then select the Close button.

There are two final steps you need to take before testing your script:

1. Select the Start button on the taskbar and choose Programs, Accessories, Internet Tools, Internet Setup Wizard to start the Internet Setup Wizard.

2. When the Internet Setup Wizard dialog box appears, step through the screens until you come to the screen that asks for the phone number of your provider. Remove the check mark from (deselect) the Bring Up Terminal Window After Dialing check box. (If the Terminal window comes up, it will interfere with your script.) Continue through the remaining screens until you can select the Finish button to resave your connection.

To test your script, launch your connection the same as you normally would, except that now the Terminal window should not appear before you connect to your provider.

If you don't connect, go back and recheck your script for any errors in spelling, capitalization, or punctuation. Check to make sure that the prompts you are waiting for are correct, and that the responses you make to the prompts are the same as those you normally type. Check again in the Setup Wizard to make sure the Bring Up Terminal Window After Dialing check box is not selected and that you entered your username and password correctly. Unfortunately, there aren't a lot of error messages that appear to direct you when something is not entered correctly, so creating your script may involve a bit of trial and error before everything clicks. Be sure to also check the Help section for **scripting**.

As an example, I have included the script file I wrote and use to log in to my provider:

```
; login script file
; city-net.scp
proc main
      waitfor "Username:", matchcase
      transmit $USERID, raw
      transmit "<cr><lf>"
      waitfor "Password:", matchcase
      transmit $PASSWORD, raw
      transmit "<cr><lf>"
      waitfor "Router>", matchcase
      transmit "PPP"
      transmit "<cr><lf>"
endproc
```

INDEX

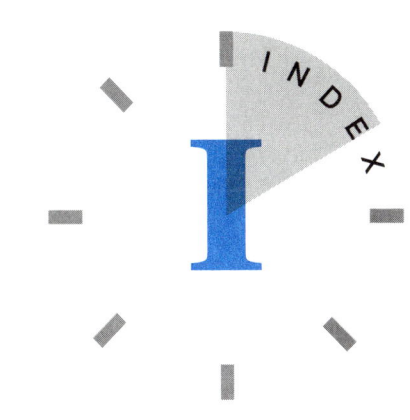

A

accounts, 4
    PPP (Point-to-Point
        Protocol), 9-10
    shell accounts, 8
    SLIP (Serial Line Internet
        Protocol) accounts, 9-10
    SLIP/PPP, configuring, 18-22
Add Bookmark command
    (Bookmarks menu), 80
Add New Hardware dialog
    box, 25
Add to Favorites command
    (Favorites menu), 85
Add/Remove Programs
    Wizard, 61
Address Book, MS Exchange,
    configuring, 52-54
addresses
    email, 28
    IP (Internet Protocol), 20
    subnet masks, 20
alt (alternative) newsgroups,
    124
Alumet Center for Education
    Online Service IRC client,
    152
America Online, 7-8
anti-virus programs, 41
ARPANET, 1

articles (newsgroups)
    posting, 136-139
    reading, 131-134
    threads, 123
ASCII files, 141
audio, playing, 105-107
Avatar digital actor, Worlds
    Chat, 146

B

binary files, 141
bionet (biology) newsgroup,
    125
bitmap files, saving, 102
biz (business) newsgroup, 125
bookmarks (Netscape), 67
    menus, creating, 82-84
    placing, 79-84
Bookmarks menu commands
    Add Bookmark, 80
    View Bookmarks, 81-82
bps (bits per second), modems,
    5
browsers
    graphic files, types, 99-104
    Internet Explorer, 36, 68-78
        attaining a copy of, 68-70
        *configuring additional file
        types, 112 113*
        running, 70-78

Netscape, 9, 60-61
   bookmarks, 67
   History feature, 67
   RealAudio, playing, 105-111

C

carbon copies, email, creating, 55-56
Carnegie Mellon University, Lycos search engine, 95-98
Casey Kasem's weekly Hit List home page, 1
categorical searches, Yahoo search engine, 91-93
chat rooms, Worlds Chat, 146
Chat Server, 152
clients, 13, 153-154
commands
   Bookmarks menu
      Add Bookmark, 80
      View Bookmarks, 81-82
   Compose menu, New Message, 55
   Favorites menu, Add to Favorites, 85
   File menu
      Exit, 103
      New Entry, 53
      Open, 71
      Open Location, 64, 118
      Save As, 102
      Save Binary Attachment, 142
   Group menu
      Show Only Subscribed Groups, 136
      Subscribe, 135
   Insert menu, Insert Header, 83
   Item menu, Properties, 81
   Options menu
      Gopher Set Up, 155
      Preferences, 110
   Post menu
      Follow Up Article, 138
      New Article, 139
   Start menu, Programs, 6
   Tools menu, Deliver Now, 56
commercial online services, 7-8, 169-173
comp (computers) newsgroups, 124
Compose menu commands, 55
composing email, MS Exchange, 54-56
compression, 10
CompuServe, 7-8
configuring
   Dial-Up Networking, 23-26
   Free Agent newsgroup, 130
   Internet Wizard, 27-34
   modems, 25
   MS Exchange, 51-52
   Netscape, 117-119
   SLIP/PPP connections, 18-22
   Worlds Chat, 147-148
Connect To dialog box, 36
connections, 5
   configuring, Internet Wizard, 27-34
   Dial-Up Networking
      configuring, 23-26
      connecting to Internet, 35-39
      scripts, 174-178
   error detection, 10
   MS Network, 169-173
   Point-to-Point Protocol (PPP), 9
   Serial Line Internet Protocol (SLIP), 9
   SLIP/PPP, configuring, 18-22
   TCP/IP (Transmission Control Protocol/Internet Protocol), 13

INDEX 181

Control Panel, 14
costs, commercial online
  services, 8, 173
courts newsgroup, 125

D

decoding binary files, UseNet,
  140-144
decompressing files, PKUNZIP,
  42
deleting network components,
  17
Deliver Now command (Tools
  menu), 56
Dial-Up Adapter, installing, 16
Dial-Up Networking
  connections
    configuring, 23-26
    connecting to Internet,
      35-39
    scripts, creating, 174-178
Dial-Up Scripting Tool dialog
  box, 177
dialog boxes
  Add New Hardware, 25
  Address Book, 53
  Connect To, 36
  DNS Server Address, 32
  Exchange Profile, 33
  Index Search, 163
  Internet Mail, 33
  IP Address, 31
  Make New Connection, 24
  Network, 14
  Open Location, 64, 118
  Options, 48
  Phone Number, 30
  Select Device, 15
  Select Network Client, 14
  Select Network Component
    Type, 14
  Service Provider
    Information, 30

Session Profile, 47
Unknown File Type, 117
User Name and Password,
  31
View Empty Group, 131
displaying
  MPEG files, 115-116
  newsgroups, 131-134
  QuickTime viewer movies,
    119-122
DNS (Domain Name Service),
  28-32
DNS Server Address dialog
  box, 32
downloading files, 40
  Free Agent newsgroup, 128
  QuickTime viewer, 118-119
  WS_FTP32, 49

E

email
  addresses, 28
  carbon copies, creating,
    55-56
  composing, 54-56
  emoticons, 57-58
  programs, 58-59
  receiving, 56-58
  sending, 54-56
  server domains, 28
Email Connection, 58
emoticons, email, 57-58
encoding binary files, UseNet,
  140-144
error detection, 10
ESPNET Sportszone home
  page, 81
Eudora email program, 58
Exchange Profile dialog box,
  33
Exit command (File menu),
  103

F

FAQs (Frequently Asked Questions), 109
Favorite Page markers (Internet Explorer), creating, 75, 84-87
Favorites menu commands, 85
File menu commands
　Exit, 103
　New Entry, 53
　Open, 71
　Open Location, 64, 118
　Save As, 102
　Save Binary Attachment, 142
files
　ASCII files, 141
　binary files, 141
　bitmap files, saving, 102
　downloading
　　FTP, 40
　　WS_FTP32, 49
　GIF files, 99
　graphic files, 99-104, 140-144
　JPEG (Joint Photographers' Expert Group) files, 99
　MPEG (Motion Picture Entertainment Group) files, 112
　script files, 178
　wallpaper files, 104
flaming, newsgroups, 137
Follow Up Article command (Post menu), 138
Forte's home page, 128
Free Agent newsreader
　articles, posting, 136-139
　configuring, 130
　dowloading, 128
　graphic files, decoding/ encoding, 141-144

newsgroups
　displaying subscribed only, 136
　flaming, 137
　netiquette, 139
　subscribing to, 135-136
FTP (File Transfer Protocol), 40-41
　downloading files, 40
　PKUNZIP file decompression program, 42
　user limits, 42
　viruses, 41
　WS_FTP32, 46-50
FTP utility, 40-45

G

Galaxy search engine, 98
gateways, 4
general newsgroups, 125
GIF files, 99
Gopher, 153
　clients, 153-154
　navigating, 156-159
　searches, 156, 160-164
　Veronica, 160-164
Gopher Set Up command (Options menu), 155
graphic files, 99-104
　saving, 99
　UseNet, 140-144
Group menu commands, 135-136
GUIs (Graphical User Interfaces), 8

H

Hampson, Martyn (HGopher) 154-156
helper apps, 117-118

HGopher, 154-156
  gopherspace, navigating, 156-159
  installing, 154-156
  Veronica searches, 161
History feature, Netscape, 67
home pages, 63
  bookmarks, placing, 79-84
  links, 66
  locating, search engines, 88-98
host names, 28
humor newsgroups, 125

I

icons, 36
Index Search dialog box, 163
Infoseek search engine, 97
inline skating Web site, 2
Insert Header command (Insert menu), 83
Insert menu commands, 83
installing
  Dial-Up Adapter, 16
  HGopher, 154-156
  Netscape, 60-61
  RealAudio, 107-111
  TCP/IP client, 13-17
  WS_FTP32, 46
Internet, 1-3
  connecting to, 35-39, 169-173
  FTP (File Transfer Protocol), 40-41
  Gopher, 153
  graphic files, 99-104
  IRC (Internet Relay Chat), 145-152
  ISPs (Internet Service Providers), 7
  UseNet, 123-124
  WWW (World Wide Web), 60-67

Internet Explorer, 68-78
  appearance, changing, 76-78
  attaining copy of, 68-70
  Favorite Page markers, creating, 75, 84-87
  file types, configuring additional, 112-113
  MPEG files, configuring to, 114-116
  RealAudio, playing, 105-107
  running, 70-78
  toolbar, 73-76
  WWW, navigating, 73-78
  Yahoo search engine, linking to, 89
Internet Mail dialog box, 33
Internet Setup Wizard
  connection configuration, 13
  running, 29-34
Internet Wizard, connections, configuring, 27-34
IP (Internet Protocol), addresses, 20, 28
IP Address dialog box, 31
IRC (Internet Relay Chat), 145-152
ISDN (Integrated Services Digital Network), 5, 11
ISPs (Internet Service Providers), 3
  accounts, 4
  MS Network, 173
  PPP (Point-to-Point Protocol) accounts, 9-10
  selecting, 7, 10-12
  shell accounts, 8
  SLIP (Serial Line Internet Protocol) accounts, 9-10
  specifications, 28
Item menu commands, 81

J-M

JHM MOO, 167
JPEG (Joint Photographers' Expert Group) files, 99
keyword searches, Yahoo search engine, 93-95
LANs (local area networks), 4
links, Web pages, 66
listing newsgroups, 131-134
Local System, WS_FTP32, 48
Lycos search engine, 95-98
Make New Connection dialog box, 24
McAfee anti-virus program, 41
Microsoft Internet Explorer Web page, 70
Microsoft Network home page, 72
Microsoft Plus!
    Dial-Up Networking connection, creating scripts, 174-178
    Internet Wizard, configuring connections, 27-34
    Microsoft Internet Explorer, 36
    TCP/IP client installation, 14
    utilities, 5
misc (miscellaneous) newsgroups, 125
modems
    configuring, 25
    system requirements, 4
MOOs (MUDs Object Oriented), 165
movies, QuickTime, displaying, 119-122
MPEG (Motion Picture Entertainment Group) files, 112
MPEG viewers, obtaining, 113-114
MS Exchange, 51-59
    Address Book, configuring, 52-54
    configuring, 51-52
    email
        carbon copies, 55-56
        composing, 54-56
        receiving, 56-58
        sending, 54-56
MS Network, 7-8, 169-170
    fees, 173
    Internet, connecting to, 169-173
    subscribing to, 170-172
    welcome screen, 171
MUDs (Multi-User Domains), 165-168
MUGs, 165
MUSEs, 165
MUSHes, 165

N

navigating
    Gopherspace, 156-159
    WWW, 62-67, 73-78
netiquette, 139
Netscape, 9, 60-61
    attaining copy of, 60-61
    Bookmarks, 67
        creating menus, 82-84
        placing, 79-84
    configuring, 117-119
    History feature, 67
    home page, 62
    installing, 60-61
    RealAudio, playing, 105-107
    toolbar, 63
    WWW, navigating, 62-67
Network dialog box, 14
New Article command (Post menu), 139

New Entry command (File menu), 53
New Message command (Compose menu), 55
New Riders' Official WWW Yellow Pages search engine, 97
news (newsgroups) newsgroup, 124
news servers, 126
newsgroups (UseNet), 123-124
   articles
      posting, 136-139
      reading, 131-134
      threads, 123
   categories, 124-125
   displaying subscribed only, 136
   downloading, 128-131
   flaming, 137
   graphic files, 140-144
   netiquette, 139
   server names, 28
   subscribing to, 135-136
newsreaders, 126
Norton Anti-Virus program, 41

O-P

online services, 169
Open command (File menu), 71
Open Location command (File menu), 64, 118
Open Location dialog box, 118
Open Text search engine, 97
Options dialog box, 48
Options menu commands
   Gopher Set Up, 155
   Preferences, 110

Paramount Pictures home page, 65
Pegasus email program, 58
Phone Number dialog box, 30

PKUNZIP, file decompression, 42
playing
   MUDs, 165-168
   RealAudio, 105-111
Post menu commands, 138-139
Post-Dial Terminal Screen window, 37
posting
   articles, 136-139
   graphic files, 143
PPP (Point-to-Point Protocol) accounts, 9-10
Preferences command (Options menu), 110
Prodigy online service, 7-8
programs
   Alumet Center for Education Online Service IRC server, 152
   Chat Server IRC server, 152
   Email Connection, 58
   Eudora email program, 58
   helper apps, 117-118
   HGopher, 154-156
   Internet Explorer browser, 70-78
   McAfee anti virus, 41
   MPEG viewers, 113-114
   Netscape Web browser, 60-67
   newsreaders, 126
   Norton Anti-Virus, 41
   Pegasus email program, 58
   PKUNZIP file decompression program, 42
   Prospero's Global Stage IRC server, 152
   Pueblo MUDs game extensions, 168
   QuickTime viewers, 119-122
   r.u.there? IRC server, 152
   RealAudio, 107-111
   Tulsa Chat IRC server, 152

VMPeg MPEG viewer, 114
Worlds Chat IRC client, 145-146
WSIRC IRC client, 151
Programs command (Start menu), 6
Properties command (Item menu), 81
Prospero's Global Stage IRC server, 152
Pueblo MUDs game extensions, 168

Q-R

QuickTime viewers, 119-122
r.u.there? IRC server, 152
reading
    email, 56-58
    newsgroup articles, 131-134
RealAudio
    FAQ page, printing, 109
    installing, 107-111
    playing, 105-111
RealAudio home page, 108
rec (recreational) newsgroup, 125
receiving email, 56-58
Reebok's home page, 80
Remote System, WS_FTP32, 48
running
    FTP utility, 41-45
    Internet Explorer, 70-78
    Internet Setup Wizard, 29-34
    Worlds Chat, 148-151
    WS_FTP32, 47-50

S

Save As command (File menu), 102
Save Binary Attachment command (File menu), 142

saving
    bitmap files, 102
    graphic files, 99
sci (science) newsgroup, 125
scripts
    Dial-Up Networking connection, creating, 174-178
    logins, 37
search engines, 88
    Galaxy, 98
    Infoseek, 97
    Lycos search engine, 95-98
    New Riders' Official WWW Yellow Pages, 97
    Open Text, 97
    WebCrawler, 97
    Yahoo, 88-95
searches, Gopher, 156, 160-164
Select Device dialog box, 15
Select Network Client dialog box, 14
Select Network Component Type dialog box, 14
sending email, MS Exchange, 54-56
service fees, commercial online services, 8
Service Provider Information dialog box, 30
service providers, see *ISPs*
Session Profile dialog box, 47
Session Profile window, WS_FTP32, 47
Setup wizard, 27
shell accounts, 8
Show Only Subscribed Groups command (Group menu), 136
SLIP (Serial Line Internet Protocol) accounts, 9-10
SLIP/PPP connections, configuring, 18-22
soc (social) newsgroup, 125

Space Station, Worlds Chat, 146
stand-alone computers, 7
Star Trek: Voyager Web page, 66
Start menu commands, 6
subnet masks, 20, 28
Subscribe command (Group menu), 135
subscribing to
    MS Network, 170-172
    newsgroups, 135-136
system requirements, Windows 95, 3-6

T-U

talk newsgroup, 125
TCP/IP (Transmission Control Protocol/Internet Protocol), 13
TCP/IP clients, 13-17
text files, 141
threads, articles, 123, 132
toolbars
    Internet Explorer, 73-76
    Netscape, 63
Tools menu commands, 56
Tulsa Chat IRC server, 152

University of Minnesota, Gopher, 153
Unknown File Type dialog box, 117
unsubscribing to newsgroups, 136
URLs (Uniform Resource Locators), 65
UseNet, 123
    articles
        posting, 136-139
        reading, 131-134
        downloading files, 128-131
        graphic files, 140-144

newsgroups, 123-124
    articles, 123
    categories, 124-125
    displaying subscribed only, 136
    flaming, 137
    netiquette, 139
    subscribing to, 135-136
newsreaders, 126
system requirements, 125-126
User Name and Password dialog box, 31

V-Z

V.42 modems, 5
Veronica, Gopher searches, 160-164
View Bookmarks command (Bookmarks menu), 81-82
View Empty Group dialog box, 131
viewing, see *displaying*
viruses, FTP, 41
VMPeg MPEG viewer, 114

wallpaper files, 104
WebCrawler search engine, 97
Windows 95
    Control Panel, 14
    system requirements, 3-6
    TCP/IP client, installing, 13-17
WinIPCfg utility, 38
Worlds Chat, 145-146
    attaining copy of, 146-148
    Avatar digital actor, 146
    chat rooms, 146
    configuring, 147-148
    Help section, 151
    running, 148-151
    Space Station, 146

WS_FTP32
    files, downloading, 49
    installing, 46
    running, 47-50
WSIRC IRC client, 151
WWW (World Wide Web), 60-67
    browsers
        graphic files, 99-104
        Internet Explorer, 68-78
        Netscape, 60-61
        playing audio, 105-107
    home pages, 63, 66
    links, 66
    navigating, 62-67
    search engines, 88-98
    URLs (Uniform Resource Locators), 65

Yahoo search engine, 88-95
    categorical searches, 91-93
    home page, 91
    keyword searches, 93-95
    search queries, 91

GET CONNECTED
to the ultimate source of computer information!

The MCP Forum on CompuServe

Go online with the world's leading computer book publisher! Macmillan Computer Publishing offers everything you need for computer success!

Find the books that are right for you!
A complete online catalog, plus sample chapters and tables of contents give you an in-depth look at all our books. The best way to shop or browse!

➤ Get fast answers and technical support for MCP books and software

➤ Join discussion groups on major computer subjects

➤ Interact with our expert authors via e-mail and conferences

➤ Download software from our immense library:
  ▷ Source code from books
  ▷ Demos of hot software
  ▷ The best shareware and freeware
  ▷ Graphics files

Join now and get a free CompuServe Starter Kit!

To receive your free CompuServe Introductory Membership, call **1-800-848-8199** and ask for representative #597.

The Starter Kit includes a personal ID number and password, a $15 credit on the system, and a subscription to *CompuServe Magazine!*

MACMILLAN COMPUTER PUBLISHING

CompuServe

Once on the CompuServe System, type:
GO MACMILLAN
for the most computer information anywhere!

PLUG YOURSELF INTO...

THE MACMILLAN INFORMATION SUPERLIBRARY™

Free information and vast computer resources from the world's leading computer book publisher—online!

FIND THE BOOKS THAT ARE RIGHT FOR YOU!
A complete online catalog, plus sample chapters and tables of contents!

- **STAY INFORMED** with the latest computer industry news through our online newsletter, press releases, and customized Information SuperLibrary Reports.
- **GET FAST ANSWERS** to your questions about Macmillan Computer Publishing books.
- **VISIT** our online bookstore for the latest information and editions!
- **COMMUNICATE** with our expert authors through e-mail and conferences.
- **DOWNLOAD SOFTWARE** from the immense Macmillan Computer Publishing library:
    - Source code, shareware, freeware, and demos
- **DISCOVER HOT SPOTS** on other parts of the Internet.
- **WIN BOOKS** in ongoing contests and giveaways!

TO PLUG INTO MCP:

WORLD WIDE WEB: **http://www.mcp.com**

FTP: ftp.mcp.com

Complete and Return this Card for a *FREE* Computer Book Catalog

Thank you for purchasing this book! You have purchased a superior computer book written expressly for your needs. To continue to provide the kind of up-to-date, pertinent coverage you've come to expect from us, we need to hear from you. Please take a minute to complete and return this self-addressed, postage-paid form. In return, we'll send you a free catalog of all our computer books on topics ranging from word processing to programming and the internet.

Mr. ☐ Mrs. ☐ Ms. ☐ Dr. ☐

Name (first) ☐☐☐☐☐☐☐☐☐☐☐☐ (M.I.) ☐ (last) ☐☐☐☐☐☐☐☐☐☐☐☐☐☐☐

Address ☐☐☐☐☐☐☐☐☐☐☐☐☐☐☐☐☐☐☐☐☐☐☐☐☐☐☐☐
☐☐☐☐☐☐☐☐☐☐☐☐☐☐☐☐☐☐☐☐☐☐☐☐☐☐☐☐

City ☐☐☐☐☐☐☐☐☐☐☐☐ State ☐☐ Zip ☐☐☐☐☐ ☐☐☐☐

Phone ☐☐☐ ☐☐☐ ☐☐☐☐ Fax ☐☐☐ ☐☐☐ ☐☐☐☐

Company Name ☐☐☐☐☐☐☐☐☐☐☐☐☐☐☐☐☐☐☐☐☐

E-mail address ☐☐☐☐☐☐☐☐☐☐☐☐☐☐☐☐☐☐☐☐☐☐☐☐☐☐☐

1. Please check at least (3) influencing factors for purchasing this book.

Front or back cover information on book .... ☐
Special approach to the content .... ☐
Completeness of content .... ☐
Author's reputation .... ☐
Publisher's reputation .... ☐
Book cover design or layout .... ☐
Index or table of contents of book .... ☐
Price of book .... ☐
Special effects, graphics, illustrations .... ☐
Other (Please specify): _____ ☐

2. How did you first learn about this book?

Internet Site .... ☐
Saw in Macmillan Computer
  Publishing catalog .... ☐
Recommended by store personnel .... ☐
Saw the book on bookshelf at store .... ☐
Recommended by a friend .... ☐
Received advertisement in the mail .... ☐
Saw an advertisement in: _____ ☐
Read book review in: _____ ☐
Other (Please specify): _____ ☐

3. How many computer books have you purchased in the last six months?

This book only .... ☐   3 to 5 books .... ☐
2 books .... ☐   More than 5 .... ☐

4. Where did you purchase this book?

Bookstore .... ☐
Computer Store .... ☐
Consumer Electronics Store .... ☐
Department Store .... ☐
Office Club .... ☐
Warehouse Club .... ☐
Mail Order .... ☐
Direct from Publisher .... ☐
Internet site .... ☐
Other (Please specify): _____ ☐

5. How long have you been using a computer?

Less than 6 months .. ☐   6 months to a year ..... ☐
1 to 3 years .... ☐   More than 3 years ...... ☐

6. What is your level of experience with personal computers and with the subject of this book?

	With PC's	With subject of book
New	☐	☐
Casual	☐	☐
Accomplished	☐	☐
Expert	☐	☐

Source Code — ISBN: 0-7897-0663-6

7. **Which of the following best describes your job title?**

Administrative Assistant .... ☐
Coordinator .... ☐
Manager/Supervisor .... ☐
Director .... ☐
Vice President .... ☐
President/CEO/COO .... ☐
Lawyer/Doctor/Medical Professional .... ☐
Teacher/Educator/Trainer .... ☐
Engineer/Technician .... ☐
Consultant .... ☐
Not employed/Student/Retired .... ☐
Other (Please specify): .... ☐

8. **Which of the following best describes the area of the company your job title falls under?**

Accounting .... ☐
Engineering .... ☐
Manufacturing .... ☐
Marketing .... ☐
Operations .... ☐
Sales .... ☐
Other (Please specify): .... ☐

9. **What is your age?**

Under 20 .... ☐
21-29 .... ☐
30-39 .... ☐
40-49 .... ☐
50-59 .... ☐
60-over .... ☐

10. **Are you:**

Male .... ☐
Female .... ☐

11. **Which computer publications do you read regularly? (Please list)**

_____
_____
_____
_____
_____
_____
_____
_____
_____

Comments: _____
_____
_____

Fold here and scotch-tape to m

ATTN MARKETING
MACMILLAN COMPUTER PUBLISHING
MACMILLAN PUBLISHING USA
201 W 103RD ST
INDIANAPOLIS IN 46209-9042

POSTAGE WILL BE PAID BY THE ADDRESSEE

BUSINESS REPLY MAIL
FIRST-CLASS MAIL PERMIT NO. 9918 INDIANAPOLIS IN

NO POSTAGE
NECESSARY
IF MAILED
IN THE
UNITED STATES